Faith & Reason

Interpretations

series editor: Roy Harris

This new series aims to explore the key concepts of intellectual enquiry in the Western world. Some of these concepts have a long and controversial history; others are of relatively recent origin. All are open to different interpretations by different thinkers.

Interpretations has two main aims:

to offer a survey of the main interpretations of an idea: those interpretations which have been influential in the history of Western thought

to offer experts an opportunity to present their own interpretation both of the idea and of its historical importance.

While giving the student an introduction to an important topic in the history of ideas, each volume in the series also represents an original contribution to that subject by a specialist in the field.

The language of the series is that of the general reader. All unfamiliar or technical terms are fully explained and critically evaluated.

Faith & Reason

Stephen Mulhall

Duckworth

First published in 1994 by
Gerald Duckworth & Co. Ltd.
The Old Piano Factory
48 Hoxton Square, London N1 6PB
Tel: 071 729 5986
Fax: 071 729 0015

A catalogue record for this book is available
from the British Library

ISBN 0 7156 2626 4

Typeset by Ray Davies
Printed in Great Britain by
Redwood Books Ltd., Trowbridge

Contents

For Paul – who liked the plot

1

The Idolatry of Reason

It did not require the advent of Enlightenment for Christianity to acknowledge the claims of reason upon the professions of faith. Aquinas' synthesis of Christian theology and Aristotelian philosophy allowed that God had revealed to the human race certain truths about himself which were not ascertainable by reason and whose acceptance therefore called for faith; but he also argued that the existence of such a revelation could be demonstrated on reason's own terms, as could the existence of, and certain other truths about, the God who had thus revealed himself. According to this specification, then, faith permitted access to truths otherwise beyond the human mind, but was not therefore in conflict with reason; on the contrary, its superior reach was underwritten in terms that reason could grasp and must acknowledge as licit.

According to the philosopher of Enlightenment, however, such an adjudication of reason's limits amounted to its abnegation. Properly – that is, critically – understood, every aspect of the divine revelation that Christ offered the human race required reason's imprimatur: 'Even the Holy One of the gospel must first be compared with our ideal of moral perfection before we can recognize him to be such ... Imitation has no place in morality, and examples serve us only for encouragement ... but they can never entitle us to set aside their

true original, which resides in reason ...'.[1] Kant's cri-
tique of practical reason thus offers us a Son of God
made in Reason's image – a simultaneous moralization
of divinity and rationalization of morality that together amount to a deification of reason; and inevitably, his refusal to cede to faith an autonomous sphere
in the human intellectual economy raises the question
what remains of the specificity of faith's object. Can
any conception of the divine succeed in passing the
tribunal of autonomous reason without being evacu-
ated of that which distinguishes the object of religious
faith from that of moral endeavour or metaphysical
speculation? Pascal had detected the risks religion
runs in courting, or even suffering, the attentions of
philosophy many years earlier: 'Even if someone were
convinced that the proportions between numbers are
immaterial, eternal truths, depending on a first truth
in which they subsist, called God, I should not consider
that he had made much progress towards his salvation'.[2] In short, the God of the philosophers is not the
God of Abraham, Isaac and Jacob: *pace* Aquinas, once
reason is permitted within the precincts of faith, it
cannot be trusted to prepare (or even to delineate) the
ground for worship but will rather construct an idol in
its own image.

In this short book, I wish to assess the significance
of certain recent developments in the philosophy of
religion against the background of this perennial dispute, with a view to ascertaining whether it is either
desirable or possible for philosophers to establish a
settlement between faith and reason according to
which each can retain its integrity without requiring
the other's subservience. In particular, I want to ask
whether any adequate philosophical account of the
Christian God and of the true nature of belief in that

God will dictate either that one must jettison, or that one must adopt, that belief, or whether its adequacy will be manifest precisely in its avoidance of any such dictation. In short: is there, between these two faces of the human spirit, any real chance of a mutual acknowledgement of otherness, an acknowledgement that does not take the form of judgement?

According to one widespread and highly influential point of view in contemporary philosophy, the idea of reason's availability as a demonstrative buttress for faith has been thoroughly discredited in the modern era. This is most evident in the manner in which the three most famous putative proofs of God's existence have been reduced to the status of paradigm cases of the abuse of human rational faculties; fledgling students of the subject are encouraged to stretch their wings by unmasking the logical frailties of the onto-logical, cosmological and design arguments.[3]

According to the standard interpretation of the onto-logical argument, attributed to Descartes and – before him – to Anselm, even those foolish enough to deny that there is a God must have grasped the commonly agreed conception of the being whose existence they are denying, a conception according to which God is something than which nothing greater can be conceived; and this idea of God must therefore exist in their understanding. Of course, many things that exist in the understanding do not exist in reality – unicorns and golden mountains, for example. But something than which nothing greater can be conceived cannot exist solely in the understanding, for to exist in reality is greater, and it would then be possible to conceive of something greater than something than which nothing greater can be conceived – namely, something that existed both in the understanding *and* in reality. Accordingly, a correct grasp of the Christian conception of 'God' entails that God exists not just in the understanding of those who dispute over his existence but also in reality.

Unfortunately, this argument presupposes that something is greater if it exists in addition to being conceived of than if it is only conceived of, i.e. that something is greater if it exists than if it does not exist, that existence is (as Descartes puts it) a perfection. And philosophers over the centuries have not tired of pointing out that this is a remarkably queer doctrine. It may be better for mankind if God exists than if he does not, but is it better for God? Is he thereby made more perfect? It makes perfect sense to say that my future word processor will be a better one if it is equipped with a hard disk than if it is not; but what could it mean to say that it will be a better word processor if it exists than if it does not? If two journalists each describe the characteristics of the person they consider to be the most perfect subject of a scandal, and the two descriptions are identical except for the fact that one specifies that the person should actually exist, have they each described a different person or type of person? *Any* person who satisfied one description would necessarily satisfy the other, and *vice versa*. In short, as Kant puts it, existence is not a real predicate; by however many predicates we define a thing, we do not make the least addition or modification to our specification of its nature when we further declare that it exists (although we may of course thereby add to our knowledge of 'the furniture of the universe'). Existence is not a perfection; it is rather that in the absence of which there is no perfection. And once this point is grasped, the ontological argument is deprived of its fulcrum.

Cosmological arguments (a species primarily associated with Aquinas, who shared the modern philosophical suspicion of the ontological argument) employ a very different strategy. They amount to suggesting that God is needed as the ultimate explanation of the way things are if intellectual enquiry is to be satisfied, that the reason why any particular thing exists must, in the end, be God. Answers in terms of what are known as secondary causes are inadequate, since no matter what cause is offered, the question of its cause can always be raised. To adapt Herbert McCabe's example,[4] we can explain Kitty's existence by reference to the existence of her parents; but that raises the question of what brought about their existence, and then in turn how the cat species evolved, and so on into a pointless infinite regress. Intellectual satisfaction demands an end to the regress, which means a cause that cannot itself be caused; and God, it is suggested, is such a cause.

As it stands, however, this argument posits an inadequacy in ordinary answers to causal questions that doesn't exist. When we respond to a child's asking 'How come Kitty?' by pointing to the older, lazy Tabitha with whom she has long been familiar, is our answer inadequate because it makes no reference to Tabitha's parents? And if, when a child asks us where she came from, we offer an accurate tale of human procreation, have we erred in failing to invoke an uncaused cause? The fact that certain other questions *could* be raised in response to our answers does not mean that they will or must be so raised, and so does not entail that the original answers are inadequate; *that* depends rather upon whether or not our answers supply the information that the questioner lacked. Furthermore, if 'God' were given as the general, ultimate answer to all our specific causal questions, it would succeed in explaining nothing, for it would offer us no additional information about any one of the specific phenomena in which we were originally interested.

Such objections typically lead to a reformulation of the original argument, one which shifts our understanding of the *explanans*: God, understood as uncaused cause, is offered to us, not as an explanation of why one specific thing rather than another occurred, but as an explanation of the existence of the world. The question to which God is the only possible answer is 'Why is there something rather than nothing?'; and that question is held to be intellectually unavoidable because it is one to which we are driven by the entirely legitimate attempt to answer any specific causal question in the manner science demands. A scientific understanding of Kitty's existence will invoke not only the existence of Tabitha and then of the cat species as such, but will also move into the realms of biochemistry, physics and so cosmology; we can and do ask, not only 'What made Kitty?', but also 'What makes Kitty a cat (as opposed to a dog)?', and 'What makes Kitty a living (as opposed to an inanimate) being?', and finally 'What makes Kitty exist (as opposed to not existing)?' We can think of this process as a matter of asking for an explanation of Kitty's existence against a progressively wider background until that background has become as wide as it is possible to get – until, that is, we ask 'How come there is a world (with cats, living and inanimate beings, and so on) at all?' To that question, no scientific answer is available, because science deals with phenomena and processes that are part of the world whose existence is in question, and so form part of the *explanandum*; to that question, God is the only possible answer.

The difficulty with this revised argument is that it presupposes that the question to which it offers God as the answer is intelligible. That question is presented as a more general form of a standard causal question: instead of asking how a certain event or entity come to be, we ask how everything came to be. But when the question is posed with respect to a particular thing, there are at least two conditions which make it possible to set about answering it: first, we can assume the existence of something other than the thing in question (to which we might relate it causally); and secondly, we can assume that the thing in question might not have existed, i.e. that its existence makes a specifiable difference to the world (for without knowing what difference the thing's existence makes we could not even begin to search for what brought it about). In short: To ask 'How come there's a fly in my soup?' is to ask 'What brought it about that this soup is not a fly-free zone?' However, neither of these conditions is met when the putative object of our explanation is 'the world'. If we ask how everything came to be, how can we appeal to something other than 'everything' to explain its existence? And if we are asked to imagine nothing rather than 'everything', to what can we appeal to specify what this alternative possible state of affairs might be?

To think that the standard type of causal question can be posed with respect to the world as a whole is to assume that the world can be regarded as a thing, or at least as a class or set of things; but this cannot be right. The members of a class satisfy the criteria for membership of that class; but there are no criteria for determining what is to count as belonging to the world. 'Everything' is not a class of things: the notion of a class entails the notion of a limit, and so of a distinction between things inside and things outside that limit;

"The world" is the answer – Hahn

but in speaking of things as being in the world, we do not mean to contrast them with other things that are (or could conceivably be) outside the world. Nor is the world a thing, as it were a great big object; it does not possess the spatio-temporal unity of an object, and there is no larger background against which we can individuate it (as we can with objects in general), determining it to be the thing it is and not another thing. If, however, it makes no sense to regard the world as a thing or class of things, it makes no sense to attempt to ask how it came to be; in other words, the question to which the cosmological argument offers God as as the only possible answer is not a genuine question at all.

The argument from design can best be thought of as a particular variant of the more general form exemplified by the cosmological argument. Both attempt to infer God's existence from certain features of the world within which we live; but whereas the cosmological argument focusses upon the fact of the world's existence, the argument from design focusses upon certain features of its structure or organization. In particular, it highlights the degree to which the various natural phenomena which go to make up that world are beautifully adapted to one another: plants are watered by rain which runs into rivers which empty themselves into the sea from which water evaporates to form clouds which water plants, bees pollinate the flowers from which they derive the raw material for their honey, predators maintain the population balance in the species that form their prey, and so on. These signs of functional interaction exactly resemble, although far exceeding in scale, the products of human intelligence and design; it is as if nature is a giant artefact. And so we can legitimately infer the existence of an

Artificer, possessed of a mind like ours but also of powers and faculties proportionate to the grandeur of his product; we can infer the existence of God.

The frailties of this argumentative strategy are not far to seek. First, its proponents ignore or repress the real ambiguity of the evidence upon which they erect their hypothesis: every sign of smoothly-functioning design in nature can be paired with a sign of malfunctioning, of droughts and desertification, disabling parasitisms, malformed organisms and self-destructive imbalances between predators and prey. If this evidence is brought into the equation, and we reason by analogy with our experience of human artefacts, we are surely bound to conclude that the divine Artificer is heavily limited in competence, intelligence and power. Secondly, the signs of functional adaptation cited above can one and all, it seems, be explained by reference to purely natural mechanisms of Darwinian selection and genetic mutation over sufficiently large stretches of time. This does not entail that the hypothesis of a divine Artificer is untenable, but it certainly shows that it can be rejected without intellectual penalty; restricting ourselves to natural explanations of natural phenomena would not deprive us of the resources needed for an adequate account of the available evidence.

Thirdly, and perhaps most important, the argument from design takes it for granted that forms of explanation employed with reference to specific worldly phenomena can be applied to the world as a whole, but without reckoning with the presuppositions of such explanations. Talk of design and construction in the case of houses and machines makes sense because we have a wide range of experience of those types of object and of the procedures needed to construct them; we can recognize a given watch as well or badly made, as half-made or complete, indeed as constructed rather than naturally produced, because we are acquainted with a wide variety of such items in a wide variety of states and with the ways in which, as well as the reasons why, they are brought into existence. But we have no such experience of a variety of universes, whether well-made, badly-made or unfinished. It is at this point that the argument from design begins to encounter the difficulties that overwhelmed its cosmological cousin. For, of course, when attempting to explain the origin of watches and houses, we can make a distinction between *explanans* and *explanandum*, and we can specify what the non-existence of the *explanandum* would amount to; but to what can we appeal when attempting to locate a candidate for the intelligent cause of the universe or to grasp the difference its existence makes? Once again, the argument from design is structured on the assumption that the world as a whole can intelligibly be treated as if it were an especially large type of object (this time an artefact); but this is incoherent. Everything is not a special sort of thing, not even a well-designed one.

It may seem that the results of this brief survey suggest that the outlook for the strategy of employing reason to legitimate the claims of faith is not bright; all of the standard arguments for God's existence are unsound. But in fact, matters are a great deal worse than this; and we can begin to see why if we examine a fourth objection to the argument from design. If that argument were sound, then God would be morally as well as physically and aesthetically responsible for every aspect of the world that he has designed. But many of the events in that world, events not directly caused by human malice, would be regarded by most human beings as bad or evil: erupting volcanoes destroy towns, children are savagely mauled by dogs bred for fighting, famines decimate the population of countries and continents. Unless we regard these things as happening contrary to God's will (thus denying his omnipotence), or without his knowledge (thus denying his omniscience), we must conclude that God is responsible for the suffering and death that is thereby inflicted on innocent human beings (thus denying his benevolence).

This is what philosophers label 'the problem of evil'. One common strategy adopted by those who wish to retain the notion of God as designer of the universe in order to solve this problem is to suggest that we must suspend judgement on this issue because we are not privy to all the relevant evidence. The reality of the suffering cited above is undeniable; but its infliction may be justified as a small element in a larger divine plan for the universe, a plan which requires this evil but only as an essential means for bringing about a far greater good for the human race in the fulness of time. Since our human perspective on the full sweep of universal history is inevitably partial and limited, we are in no position to determine whether or not such a divine plan, in terms of which the evil that we can perceive could be given a justification, exists; we can therefore conclude neither that such suffering is utterly, eternally and irredeemably pointless, nor that it is not. Consequently, we can legitimately give God the benefit of the doubt, and so avoid the trilemma specified above.

What makes this strategy not so much misbegotten as offensive is the fact that it amounts to a defence of God on the grounds that the suffering we see around us may not be haphazard – the result of natural and

essentially meaningless causal processes – but
planned, and planned on an infinitely large scale. This
apologia for God urges us to see the suffering of a
starving child as something deliberately inflicted, part
of a design hatched at the beginning of eternity and
flawlessly executed at the appointed moment; it urges
us, in other words, to comfort ourselves with the
thought that God's motivation is more deeply evil than
we might otherwise have imagined. This defence of
God attempts to justify such actions in terms of their
consequences; but it fails to see that the actions it is
concerned with, actions such as killing the innocent,
are ones we should condemn no matter what the consequences. No good, however large, could legitimate
such evil; and to attempt to do so merely deepens that
evil. As Dostoevsky's Ivan Karamazov argues in his
famous conversation with his brother:

> ... If the sufferings of children go to swell the sum
> of sufferings which was necessary to pay for truth,
> then I protest that the truth is not worth such a
> price ... I don't want harmony. From love of hu-
> manity I don't want it ... Besides, too high a price
> is asked for harmony; it's beyond our means to pay
> so much to enter on it.[5]

It is all too clear what has gone wrong here; and it
goes wrong from the moment that we identify the
difficulty here as a 'problem'. Problems are intellectual
puzzles, and they require intellectual solutions; so we
allow our rational faculties to set about constructing
an ingenious solution, and fail to notice that we have
detached ourselves thereby from even the most basic
moral sensitivity. More precisely, we find that, as part
of an attempt to absolve God from moral condemna-

tion, our reason constructs an image of God as a moral criminal, an evil demon. In other words, in this so-called rational defence of faith, reason is not just being asked to do something beyond its powers; it ends up corrupting the faith it is supposed to defend and defiling its object. Such a justification of the ways of God to man amounts to little less than blasphemy.

And what comes out most clearly when defenders of faith are pushed to this extremity is no less central to their manner of deploying all the arguments in their rational armoury. With respect to both the cosmological argument and the argument from design, we have seen that their central flaw is a failure to perceive that modes of reasoning applicable to phenomena within the world cannot be applied to the world as a whole; to do so amounts to treating the universe as if it were a thing or set of things, a great big object. But of course, both arguments involve picturing the world as an effect of some cause; so if they regard the effect in intra-worldly terms, they will also regard what they posit as the cause of that world in intra-worldly terms. If the world is understood as if it were a great big object, then the being who constructs it or brings it about must in essence be understood as if it too were a physical entity – even if possessed of unusually extensive powers.

A precisely analogous point holds with respect to the ontological argument. As we saw, this pivots on the idea that existence is a perfection: since God, the being than which nothing greater can be conceived, must necessarily be possessed of all perfections, he must necessarily exist. But when the proponents of this argument set about explaining why they view existence as a perfection, they invoke examples of ordinary physical objects: Anselm talks of a painting, suggesting that its existence in reality after the painter has com-

pleted his task is obviously greater than when it exists
merely in the painter's understanding. Of course, they
then go on to argue that God differs from any such
object, in that the idea of God's existing only in the
understanding is inconsistent with our conception of
God's nature; but the sort of existence that they then
attribute to God as one of his necessary properties is
not so distinguished from the existence they attribute
to physical objects. The real existence that he necessarily possesses is an existence in the real world, the
world of physical objects such as paintings; he is one
more item that we are licensed to place on our inven-
tory of the furniture of the universe, even if our grounds
for so doing are very different (conceptual rather than
sensory). But this amounts to treating God as if he
were just a rather special type of entity, one object or
being amongst others.

What matters about this common assumption from
a religious point of view is not its logical flaws but its
spiritual ones. In the book of Exodus, while Moses is
communing with God on Mount Sinai, the Israelites
persuade Aaron to supervise the construction of a
golden calf; and when Moses returns clutching the
stone tablets upon which the ten commandments are
inscribed, he finds them worshipping this new deity.
Moses' wrath is plainly presented as kindled not just
by the evidence this provides of the frailty of their
commitment to the one true God; for the first of the ten
commandments he brings them states not just that the
Israelites should have no other God but Jahweh, but
also that they should make unto themselves no graven
images. In other words, the construction of the golden
calf symbolises both the human impulse to worship
false gods and the impulse to construct some sort of

representation of the divine; and the God of Judaeo-Christianity sets his face implacably against both.

Of the two, it seems plausible to claim that the latter impulse has proved the most ineradicable: As George Steiner has argued in *In Bluebeard's Castle*, the aspect of Christian monotheism that has proved most difficult for the human spirit to bear is the prohibition on making images of the divine; God's self-definition – 'I am that Am' – repels the imagination, leaving nothing upon which to focus in the struggle to observe his other commandments. But what the priority of that prohibition within those commandments implies is the depth of the spiritual dangers that such representations of the divine are held to embody; it suggests that any such representation would inevitably be a misrepresentation, that it would blur the fundamental difference between the divine nature and the essentially finite resources upon which human attempts to picture that nature must draw. Directing worship to a graven image could never amount to worshipping the true God, because no property of the image could be a property of that which it is designed to represent, and *vice versa*; such an object, precisely because it is an object, would necessarily misrepresent God.

It is therefore both unsurprising and deeply disturbing to find the defenders of faith by reason offering proofs for God's existence which presuppose that the divine nature can be understood on the model of spatio-temporal phenomena, as if God were a kind of physical entity (however special a kind). On the one hand, the human need for graven images is so deep-rooted that it is unsurprising to find intellectual versions of the golden calf appearing in theology and the philosophy of religion; those possessed of intellectual skills and interests don't thereby shed their all too human nature. On the other hand, the essentially idolatrous nature of these central and time-hallowed products of the intellectual impulse in religion, the realization that such influential and perennially-renewed attempts to employ reason as the servant of faith amount to a violation of the first commandment, forces us to ask whether it is the intellectual impulse itself that is essentially idolatrous. Can religion ever regard the claims of reason as anything other than a temptation to break faith with God?

2

The Life of Truth

According to the nineteenth-century philosopher
Johannes Climacus,[6] reason is doubly incapable of
grasping the true nature of faith: first, because reason
has an inherent tendency to interpret religious belief
on the model of empirical belief, and secondly, because
the truth of Christianity is necessarily and absolutely
offensive to reason. In this chapter we will explore the
first of these claims; the second will form the topic of
Chapter Three.

When two people disagree over a matter of fact, there
are certain familiar ways in which the dispute can
usually be decided. If, for example, it turns on the
whereabouts of a particular object, then both parties
will – if they are competent to engage in the dispute in
the first place – know what sort of evidence will settle
the matter and how it might be unearthed. In deciding
whether or not our pet budgerigar has decamped to the
neighbour's apple tree, we know that establishing that
the bird on the bough has those familiar but unusual
eye-markings will support the hypothesis, whereas
finding the cage in the living room to be fully occupied
will count against it. If the dispute is over a matter of
historical fact, then similar principles apply: if we
understand the claim under dispute (e.g. that Napo-
leon died on St Helena), then we know what sort of
evidence will be pertinent to determining its truth

(eye-witness testimony, medical documents, the subsequent actions of those affected by such an event), and we know, in general, how to set about unearthing it (the usual scholarly techniques of exploring and evaluating the many available layers of textual evidence).

Such empirical contexts are the ones in which we most often meet the term 'belief'; so when we are presented with expressions of *religious* belief and are asked to assess their validity, we naturally tend to treat them as if they were a species of empirical belief, and assume that their validity turns on the sorts of evidence, and so upon the sorts of technique for uncovering and assessing evidence, with which we are familiar in empirical contexts. We assume, for example, that when Christians say 'I believe in God', their belief in God's existence is to be evaluated in just the terms in which we evaluate any existential claim, any claim about a matter of fact; and when they say 'I believe in the Incarnation', their belief must rest on grounds of the sort that are pertinent whenever someone claims that a particular person lived, performed certain actions and died at a specific point in history.

We saw at the end of the previous chapter that the attempt to comprehend the existence and nature of God in terms whose primary application is to physical objects results in logical and spiritual confusions. What Climacus does in the first part of his *Concluding Unscientific Postscript* is to make a precisely parallel argument with respect to the seemingly historical claims upon which Christianity distinctively rests – claims about Christ's birth, life and death. Given the degree to which the authority of Christian religious teaching is derived from the authority of Christ, it seems undeniable that faith in those teachings must depend upon the validity of certain historical claims about Christ's existence, about the origin and unbroken tradition of the Church and about the accumulation of divinely-inspired testimony over the years. This in turn would suggest that the question of whether one should become a Christian is ultimately to be settled by the deliverances of the usual scholarly techniques for assessing historical hypotheses – in this case the results of investigations by Bible scholars, archaeologists and Church historians.

Climacus' view is that this chain of seemingly-innocuous assumptions leads to a set of ludicrous conclusions. It implies, for example, that an individual's decision about becoming a Christian will in effect be taken by someone else – by whichever scholar or group of scholars is taken to be the most reliable and expert in this field; that that individual will be forced to alter her religious beliefs, or at least to revise the degree of her conviction in them, as the scholarly consensus changes; and that, for as long as the scholars fail to establish a consensus, she must suspend judgement, unable for much if not all of her life to determine what she should believe about Christianity and Christ. Climacus sums up the central difficulty that these examples reveal by saying that 'the greatest attainable certainty with respect to anything historical is a mere approximation'. In other words, with respect to any factual claim, any claim based on historical or other forms of empirical evidence no matter how firm, doubt can never be entirely excluded; but the kind of necessity that has traditionally been claimed for Christian teaching, the full and unconditional faith in Christ that is demanded by that religion, precisely does exclude doubt. Accordingly, Christian faith cannot rationally be grounded upon historical or, more generally, upon empirical evidence.

There are good reasons for doubting the general
validity of Climacus' claim about the inexpungeability
of doubt in the context of historical and empirical
claims. If my mother's claim to have been born on 7
July 1933 is confirmed by her parents, the hospital
records and her birth certificate, is there really any
reason to think that the facts of this matter have not
been established with certainty? It is of course true
that the converse of any such empirical claim is con-
ceivable, that the possibility of uncovering further
evidence that will cast doubt on its truth is not logically
excluded; but this is to say nothing more than that all
such claims are bipolar, capable of being true and
capable of being false – and the logical possibility of
something's being false is not in itself a ground for
doubting its truth. Within the context of empirical
claims, then, the concept of certainty has application,
serving to distinguish propositions whose grounding is
as solid as can be desired from those whose grounding
is not; and where it does have application, we can
perfectly intelligibly and perfectly rationally talk of
having excluded doubt.

Nonetheless, the true force of Climacus' argument
remains; for the ludicrousness he identifies in the
philosopher's picture of the rational approach to religious belief is not eradicated by acknowledging the
worry just outlined. Imagine, for example, that the
veracity of most of the Gospel narratives had, by the
standards appropriate to the disciplines of Biblical
scholarship, been established with certainty: would a
wavering believer in the Incarnation, in the fully divine authority of a particular, fully human being, have
been brought one step closer to faith? And if we imagine the reverse – a case in which the untrustworthiness
of the Gospel accounts had been demonstrated to the

utmost satisfaction of all Biblical scholars. – does it
follow that Christ did not exist, and so that the believer
in Christ must relinquish his belief in the Incarnation?
Climacus believes that it would be ludicrous to answer
either of these questions in the affirmative, but that
cannot be because he thinks empirical evidence is
never *enough* to license the claim to certainty that
Christians make; for that would presuppose that what
is needed is more of the same, i.e. that affirmations of
religious beliefs are of the same general epistemic
species as affirmations of empirical beliefs. And on
such a model, the realisation that religious believers
generally do not adjust their commitments according
to the fluctuating state of the empirical evidence, that
they in fact maintain a degree of commitment that no
amount of empirical evidence could license, would entail a dismissal of their claims to be acting rationally;
the ludicrousness of the situation would then be locat-
able in the religious practices themselves. But for
Climacus, what is ludicrous is not those practices but
the terms in which philosophers attempt to understand
them. What the undeniable lack of correspondence
between the commitment of the religious believer and
the supposedly pertinent historical evidence reveals is
that that historical evidence is not in fact pertinent at
all (at least, not in the same way), that religious beliefs
do not have an empirical basis; it reveals that the
evidence for religious beliefs, the doubts to which they
may be subject and the certainty they may command
are not species of empirical evidence, empirical doubts
and empirical certainty. Those concepts function in the
realm of religious belief in a manner that is entirely
different from their use in the realm of empirical belief
– which means that the concept of 'belief' is very
different in these two realms. In other words, the

impression of ludicrousness derives from the mismatch between the conceptual structures that shape those practices and those (derived from empirical contexts) in terms of which philosophers attempt to understand them.

For Climacus, the tendency of philosophers to misinterpret religion in this particular way is a very deeply rooted one – a tendency that derives from their commitment to what he calls an objective understanding of truth. Philosophy has always understood itself as engaged in a reason-guided search for truth; and it has, for almost as long, understood truth in a way that Climacus summarises as 'the agreement of thinking and being'. In more modern terms, this might be thought of as an agreement of thought and reality: to ask whether a thought or proposition is true is to ask whether or not things are as it claims them to be. It then seems to follow that to be interested in the truth of a given proposition, to be interested in whether or not one should believe it and with what degree of conviction, just is to be interested in whether or not it corresponds to reality. And since what counts as the correct answer to that question is independent of the specific identity and circumstances of the person asking it, our interest in it can be thought of as an impersonal or objective one.

Climacus wishes to deny nothing of this; but he does wish to claim that it is a partial account of truth – an account that captures only the objective side of the question. For of course, even in the case of an ordinary empirical hypothesis, our interest in whether it corresponds to reality is not just a purely cognitive or epistemic interest in acquiring an accurate picture of reality; it also has a practical or subjective side. We want to know how things are in the world because we

have to act in it; and if we can establish that a certain
picture of a particular state of affairs is the correct one,
then we can successfully employ it to guide our actions
and thus achieve what we want to achieve in relation
to it. If I establish that it is raining, then I will go
shopping only with an umbrella and only after remov-
ing the washing from the line; once I learn which
position of the gear-lever corresponds to which gear, I
can drive the car. Here, what is of interest to people is
not just the relation between the proposition and reality, but also that between the subject and the proposition: once its objective truth is established, it is
incorporated into the life of the subject – or as Climacus
would say, it acquires subjective reality by being made
manifest in an essentially practical and personal way.
An exclusive focus on the objective side of things, such
as philosophy's self-image inculcates, thus in effect
represses the fact that human beings are not free-
floating consciousnesses, would-be mirrors of a reality
that is simply presented to them, but rather embodied
agents with a life to lead in the world. It represses the
fact that truth and truth-seeking have existential implications.   *to derive meaning*
    And of course, there are certain species of truth or
belief with respect to which these subjective or existential implications are much more obviously highlighted
– those of ethics. Climacus has a broad definition of the
ethical realm, one which includes any answer to the
question of how one should live; and according to him,
what is distinctive about human existence is that each
individual constantly faces such questions – that, in
effect, to lead a human life just is to face the question
of how to do so. Possessed of mind or consciousness
as well as body, humans in addition possess self-
consciousness: they relate to their psycho-physical

existence in time in such a way that the manner of its continuation is an issue for them, something over which they can exercise real if limited influence. At each moment, they choose which of the several available possible modes of existence will be actualized – whether to act, and if so how to act, remembering always that to decide not to act is itself the actualization of one possibility; and remembering also that the same necessity to choose will recur at every moment (until death is encountered or solicited). It is the business of ethics to provide guidance for such choices – to specify a standard against which any and all of the available options can be judged as good or evil (or at least as contrary or not contrary to the good), and to require the actualization of the good.

Plainly, on this understanding of ethics, ethical beliefs are ones in which the objective facet of truth is recessive and its subjective facet dominant. While their claim to truth presupposes a claim to objectivity in the sense that they claim to articulate a requirement that really does apply impersonally to all, the fact that they are articulated in the form of a requirement shows that they explicitly confront and engage with the fact that human beings each have a life to lead. If, however, the significance of such beliefs lies manifestly in their imposition of an existential requirement, in the shape of the lives that they command those who accept them to lead, then any discipline constitutionally inclined to comprehend truth in objective terms is liable systematically to misinterpret that significance. But in fact, the deleterious consequences of philosophy's doomed attempt to understand subjective truths are far more widely-ramifying than this. For, from the point of view of the ethical, the decision to engage in philosophical work is itself an existential choice, and so one which must be measured against the requirements ethics imposes; but insofar as philosophy encourages its adherents to search for truth objectively understood, and so to adopt a purely cognitive relation to their activities, it encourages them to lead a life in which the question of their own relation to that life is not so much wrongly answered as factored out. In short, it encourages them to repress or forget the fact that they too are existing human beings, tempting them to live a life in flight from living, to haunt their own existence.

It is important to see that this forgetfulness of existence is, on Climacus' view, manifest not just in the truth-seeking side of philosophical study but also in its truth-conveying side. For, of course, philosophers are committed to communicating the truths that they claim to have established, and communication is as much a species of action — and so as much open to ethical assessment — as is reading other philosophers' writings or contemplating propositions. Now, given the philosophical focus on objective truth, the appropriate mode of communicating such truth to others will be as objective and impersonal as the appropriate modes of assessing its validity: if the investigating subject's relation to a given hypothesis is deemed entirely irrelevant to the question of its correspondence with reality, then the answer to that question not only can but should be conveyed to other subjects in a way which reflects its objectivity and impersonality. This is why, in the empirical sciences, the question of the validity of a hypothesis can be entirely detached from questions of the personal authority of its original discoverer and from the particular path by means of which she discovered it; the only point at issue is whether the proposition matches reality, and if it does then it does for anyone and everyone regardless of who they are or

Truth tries to take humans out of it. [margin handwritten note]

what they may think about the matter. And that is why
the usual mode of communicating truth in philosophy
tends to be in the form of propositions whose truth is
demonstrable by argument: the truth of the proposition rests on the validity of the argument, and both
matters are entirely insensitive to the particular identity both of those communicating the truth and of those
to whom the truth is being communicated. In this
sense, philosophy's rhetorical ideal is a form of communication in which the issue of the relation between the
particular teacher and/or the particular learner and
the propositional content of the communication is entirely suppressed in favour of that of the relation between the proposition and reality.

It is important to see that this rhetorical model is
not rejected by Climacus as entirely misbegotten; on
the contrary, when what is being communicated is an
empirical truth, such a communicational form is not
only permissible but desirable, since the aspect of its
truth that is primarily at issue really is objective and
impersonal. When, however, the subject-matter of the
philosophical investigation is an ethical proposition,
matters are very different. For here, that which is
being investigated is an existential requirement, one
which is essentially concerned with subjective truth;
its focus is the issue of how to live, and its aim is to
convince people that they should each make that choice
in the light of certain standards or ideals, and so give
a particular form to their individual existence. If such
a message is conveyed in the form of a set of propositions or hypotheses, expressed as impersonally as possible, then the form of that communication will
fundamentally conflict with the essence of its intended
content; for the use of that form will imply that the
question of the message's truth is a purely cognitive or

epistemic matter rather than an existential one, that
one might recognize its truth without allowing that
truth to make a difference to one's life, without actualizing the particular existence-possibility it represents,
without living its truth. Such an objective or direct
mode of communication, by repressing the issue of the
teacher's and the learner's personal relation to what is
being communicated, effectively represses the very
question to which the ethical teaching is intended to be
an answer.

We can therefore conclude that ethical truth cannot
be properly understood or communicated in objective
terms; and from that it follows not only that anyone
who attempts to communicate such truths in such
terms thereby manifests her misunderstanding of
what she is communicating, but also, and more importantly, that she thereby manifests her own failure to
live up to – to live – that truth. For insofar as she claims
to accept that ethical vision, she takes on the obligation
to ensure that her life as a whole reflects or embodies
it; but if she chooses to communicate that vision in a
form which not only implies that her interlocutor's
relation to it should be exclusively cognitive but also
determines her own relation to it as impersonal and
epistemic, then her communicative act at once fails to
convey that its topic is a subjective existential possibility, and itself amounts to a failure to actualize that
possibility. In short, the form of her words reveals that
their content condemns her.

This double disability – philosophy's blindness to the
true nature of the ethical and to the ethical dimension
of the deeds that are integral to existence as a philosopher – is exacerbated when philosophy attempts to
comprehend and convey the truth of Christianity. On
Climacus' view, Christianity is related to the domain

of the ethical, in that its primary concern is to provide
an answer to the question of how to live; and this focus
on the existential or subjective aspect of truth entails
that an objectively-oriented philosophical investigation will fail to grasp its essence and manifest a failure
to live up to its demands. But the difficulty is heightened because of Christ. Any ethical teaching demands
what one might call existential resolution – it asks that
its adherents live its truth; but in the case of Christianity, the truth it claims to possess is inherent in the
figure of the incarnate God-man. And this means not
that Christ possesses knowledge that humans lack but
need, and not even that his teachings articulate the
truth, but rather that he *is* the truth. After all, Christ
does not claim that he and he alone knows the way, the
truth and the life; his claim is that 'I *am* the way, the
truth and the life' – from which it follows that, in
Christian terms, establishing a relation to the truth
means establishing a relation to the person of Christ.
Since, however, it is also part of the Christian message
as Climacus understands it that human beings are
incapable of establishing such a relationship by means
of their own efforts – since human nature is sinful, and
so not so much oriented away from the truth as mired
in untruth – they must rely upon Christ not only to
initiate that personal relationship but also to put them
in a position from which such an orientation to the
truth is even possible. In short, human beings require
conversion or re-birth as well as re-orientation, and
both require grace – a gratuitous, entirely undeserved
and purely loving move on the part of Christ to come
into contact with them. (I shall return to the themes of
this paragraph in more detail in Chapter Five.)

What does this entail about any attempt to articulate or communicate the truth of Christianity? To begin

with, insofar as Christianity demands existential resolution, one must attempt to communicate the fact that
its aim is to advocate a certain answer to the question
of how to live one's life – which means finding a communicative form that appropriately reflects the fact
that it is an existential possibility rather than a set of
propositions, and that it requires individuals to relate
to that possibility as something that demands actualization rather than contemplation. However, insofar as
the truth of Christianity is Christ, this communicative
form must reflect the fact that what Christianity requires is a relationship with an actual person, i.e. not
just with an existential possibility but also with a
particular historical individual who is also God incarnate. And insofar as human beings are understood as
mired in untruth, Christianity understands the possibility of their even grasping the need to establish a
personal relation with Christ as itself requiring a
divinely-initiated re-birth, the annihilation of their old
nature and the taking on of a new one through the
action of grace. So the form in which we communicate
the Christian truth must also reflect the fact that its
demands will seem to the unconverted to amount to
self-destruction, to the denial of everything their nature requires and the death of what they take themselves to be. It is against this extremely rigorous
standard that Climacus asks us to judge his own efforts
in the later stretches of the *Postscript*, a task to which
we will now turn.

3

The Absurdity of Philosophy[7]

It is typically assumed that the second part of the *Postscript* unveils Climacus' best attempt to communicate the truth of Christianity in a form that is sensitive to the requirements specified at the end of the previous section, and that in so doing he makes use of two main lines of argument. These often rely rather too heavily for modern tastes upon the Hegelian vocabulary that permeated Climacus' philosophical *milieu*, but their underlying structure and basic plausibility can still be discerned. One rests upon a certain interpretation of the nature of the question existence poses to human beings, and the other involves a particular deployment of the linked concepts of contradiction, absurdity and nonsense.

Climacus develops the first of these arguments by suggesting that the nature of human existence ineliminably faces us with the question of what, if anything, gives meaning to our lives as a whole. At each moment of our lives we confront the question of how we should relate ourselves to the coming moment, and this requires us to locate something (some standard or value) in relation to which that choice might intelligibly be made and thus acquire any meaning; and insofar as the standard is intended to govern each and every such choice and the moments to which they refer, it can be thought of as conferring significance on that life as a whole. One type of answer to this question invokes a specific goal or achievement, such as power, wealth, or the development of a talent; and the meaning of life understood in this way is determined by our success in achieving the relevant goal. This is what Climacus regards as an aesthetic response; and since the goals it invokes only have significance because and insofar as the person concerned desires them, what gives meaning to a life in aesthetic terms lies in the subject's given array of wants and dispositions. However, such dispositions can alter; if I cease to desire riches, I will no longer live my life in accordance with the goal of achieving wealth, but will rather turn to some other of my dispositions to guide my behaviour. But that implies a founding role in my life for choice, for the exercise of my will, and so implies a certain necessary self-deception in the aesthetic attitude; despite the fact that I must choose among my dispositions, I claim to lead a life whose form is determined by whatever desires I happen to have. And upon further reflection, I will see that no such contingent aspect of my nature could conceivably provide an adequate answer to the question of the meaning of my life as a whole, because any such disposition might change, but the question would remain.

It might therefore appear that the way to resolve the difficulty is to concentrate on the capacity which really conferred meaning on my life even in the aesthetic mode of existence – my capacity for choice. In other words, I can choose in terms of my capacity for choice, and thereby impress myself upon whatever contingency I encounter, transforming the conditional into the unconditional. I might, for example, relate to my sexual impulses by choosing an unconditional commitment to marriage, or freely commit myself to one of my talents by choosing to relate to it as a vocation; I thereby choose not to permit changes in these contingencies to alter the shape of my life, maintaining its unity and integrity regardless of fluctuations in the intensity of my desires, and thereby creating a self for myself from myself.

This is the ethical mode of existence; but Climacus suspects a hidden complicity between it and the aesthetic. The ethical attitude understands my capacity for making and holding unconditionally to a choice as the source of my life's meaning; but that capacity, just insofar as it is a capacity, is still a part of my life, and so a part of that which has to be given meaning as a whole. But no part can give meaning to the whole of which it is a part; with respect to it, as with respect to any of my given desires and dispositions, I can still ask: what confers meaning on *it*?

What this implies is that the question that life sets us is not answerable in terms of anything in that life; life cannot determine its own significance in terms of itself. And according to Climacus, I am then compelled to realize that meaning can only be given to one's life as a whole by relating it to something outside it; for it is only to something outside it that my life can be related *as a whole*. Only such a standard could give a genuinely unconditional answer to the question of the meaning of one's life; only by relating ourselves to such an absolute Good, only by relativising the importance of finite (and so conditional) goods, can we properly answer the question that existence forces us to face. And such an absolute Good is, on Climacus' view, just another name for God; we can relate properly to each moment of our existence only by relating our lives as a whole to God.

The superiority of the religious mode of existence

could hardly, it seems, be more firmly established. But
to establish the need for belief in God is not yet to
establish the need to become a Christian; that involves
what Climacus calls the transition from religiousness
'A' to religiousness 'B', and his most notorious argument for the superiority of the latter rests upon his
perception of its absolute paradoxicality. On Climacus'
view, human existence itself is essentially paradoxical:
the elements of mind and body, of thought and being,
to which our self-consciousness relates us, never har-
monize but rather constantly tend to pull apart from
one another. Our minds pull us away from actuality
towards the realm of possibility: thought understands
concrete particulars in terms of universal categories,
norms which seem no more capable of fully capturing
particularity than they are of being concretely embodied (to grasp the concept of a circle is not to grasp the
existence of that circular plate on the table, but then
no plate can ever be perfectly circular). Our bodies pull
us from possibility to actuality: our needs and desires
impel action, and so impel thought to guide action by
determining which of the many existential possibilities
from which we can choose will best serve our interests.
But of course, even a successfully realized action requires will as well as thought; and one such perform-
ance cannot achieve a permanent integration of mind
and body, but rather provides a position from which we
face the next demand for a decision to actualize an
existential possibility. In short, our psycho-physical
existence sets us an endless task of struggling to resolve the irresoluble, to relate the incommensurable.

According to Climacus, coming to understand these
practical decisions, and so our existence, in an ethical
or religious light intensifies these contradictions. As
Kant's moral philosophy captures so well, when hu-

man beings come to relate to their actions in a more than purely instrumental way, their experience of the requirement to actualize the good is of an unremitting, unconditional imperative, an unyielding pressure against the flesh and its impulses exerted by a law rooted in a realm beyond the contingencies of time and space. This amounts to a redoubling of the contradictory pull of that side of our identity which has access to the eternal against our immersion as embodied beings in nature's causal flow. It thus intensifies what Climacus calls the passion of the existing subject in two senses of that term. First, it raises the stakes of existence, telling us that not just the satisfaction of our contingent wants and desires but the possibility of our eternal happiness or well-being (the *summum bonum*) is at issue throughout our lives, and thus intensifying our interest in the task of living. Secondly, it heightens the contradictions within which we have our being, intensifying and so clarifying our suffering awareness of who and what we are – of the fact that to exist is to suffer contradiction without explanation, to struggle with an impossible but unavoidable task that we neither chose nor deserved. In other words, the demand that individuals relate themselves from the perspective of finitude to an infinite requirement calls forth from them a more intense and a more pure awareness of their true situation; the paradoxicality of such a relationship echoes and resonates with the essentially contradictory nature of human existence. In an important sense, anything less paradoxical would be inappropriate.

Climacus' view of Christianity is that its distinctiveness, and its distinctive virtue, lies in the fact that its truth carries that paradoxicality to an absolute pitch, and so corresponds most perfectly to the passionate

paradoxicality of human existence. For according to
Christian teaching, finite individuals must relate
themselves to the eternal; but the eternal is understood no longer as being located outside space and time
but as being incarnate, as entering space, time and
history as a fully human individual. Any relation between the finite and the eternal is a paradoxical relation, but the eternal in itself can be understood in
non-paradoxical terms (as in the case of the Kantian
moral law); but to demand that the finite individual
relate to infinity incarnate in finitude is to render both
the relation and the object of the relation paradoxical
– it is to generate absolute paradoxicality. For if the
idea that the eternal might relate to the temporal is
contradictory, the idea that it might itself become fully
temporal while remaining fully eternal, that it might
become simultaneously infinite and finite, is absolutely contradictory.

To demand that finite individuals relate themselves
to an actual individual possessed of such a contradictory nature is to realize both contradictions simultaneously and so to purify to its fullest possible extent our
awareness of what we suffer simply by virtue of existing; for here, the very object of our concern reflects back
to us in heightened form the essence of our own nature
– its rivenness and its unity. And to claim that an
individual's eternal happiness depends upon her establishing and maintaining such a paradoxical relation to a paradoxical object amounts to calling upon her
to stake an infinite interest on an absurdity – a claim
that is perfectly designed to elicit the utmost degree of
passionate concern for the task that each moment of
life represents; for the depth of the spiritual significance that is thereby attached to this absurdity will
ensure that the mind is continually drawn back to it in

a hopeless attempt to comprehend the incomprehens-
ible. Climacus invites us to think of what is happening
here, when Christ's Passion elicits our passion, as the
infinite accentuation of the subjective side of truth;
whereas intelligible and plausible empirical hypotheses emphasise objectivity and make the subjectivity
of truth of vanishing importance, a paradox renders
objective assessments problematic and so restores a
breathing space for subjective concerns, and an absolute paradox entirely evacuates any possibility of con-
cerning oneself with the proposition's relation to
reality and so leaves nothing but subjectivity at issue.
Only an absolute absurdity can remove any admixture
of concern with the 'what' (the content) of one's belief,
and entirely direct one to a concern with the 'how' of
one's relation to it; only a claim that one's eternal
happiness rests on relating to an object whose nature
repels objective thought can elicit an infinitely passionate interest in one's existence. And on Climacus' view,
that is precisely what makes Christianity the only
adequate teaching for those whose essentially contradictory existence condemns them to a passionate concern for the significance of each of its moments.

> If, however, subjectivity is truth, and subjectivity
> is the existing subjectivity, then, if I may put it
> this way, Christianity is a perfect fit. Subjectivity
> culminates in passion, Christianity is paradox;
> paradox and passion fit each other perfectly, and
> paradox perfectly fits a person situated in the
> extremity of existence.[9]

Both of Climacus' arguments have a dialectical
steeliness that compels philosophical admiration; but
they also offer real causes for concern. In the case of

the absurdity argument, Climacus concludes that the
superiority of the Christian conception of truth rests
on its being maximally repellent to reason; it tran-
scends the merely paradoxical nature of any and all
ethical demands by defining the source of those demands as itself paradoxical. But this conclusion presupposes the possibility of making a distinction
between two types of nonsense or absurdity – the
merely paradoxical, and the absolutely paradoxical;
and this creates two major difficulties. First, is it really
possible to make distinctions within the class of the
absurd or nonsensical? Can we really talk about degrees of nonsense, or set about ranking 'thoughts' according to the degree of their nonsensicality? For
remember, 'absurd' here does not mean 'implausible':
it means 'repellent to reason', a violation of logic. And
do we really want to say that a 'thought' that combines
two contradictions is twice as nonsensical – or even
more nonsensical than – a 'thought' that embodies only
one? Is the proposition 'Green ideas sleep furiously'
twice (or is it four times?) as nonsensical as 'Green
ideas are difficult to grasp', or is the latter somehow
not entirely nonsensical? The fact that, with a different
subject, the second proposition would make sense does
not entail that, with the subject it now has, it makes
partial sense, or is less than wholly nonsensical; and
by the same token, correcting one of the deformities of
the first proposition does not make it less unintelligible
as a whole ('Difficult ideas sleep furiously' is no less
nonsensical). Both are simply, flatly and entirely nonsensical; one violation of the rules of logical syntax is
enough to empty a proposition of all content, to remove
its claim to be a proposition at all. The second worry is
even more damaging for Climacus; for even assuming
that the distinction he requires is an intelligible one,

by what means are we supposed to draw it other than those of reason? How can we distinguish between the degrees to which two given propositions are repellent to reason except by the use of reason? But then the believer must retain her understanding in order to be able to believe against the grain of her understanding; she must rely upon reason in order to identify and embrace a doctrine whose sole claim to superiority rests on its ability to be absolutely repellent to reason.

The difficulties are no less evident with respect to Climacus' other line of argument, which presents belief in God as the only adequate answer to the question of the meaning of one's life as a whole. Once again, the central problem has to do with the intelligibility of the ranking procedure upon which the argument is erected. According to him, the aesthetic mode of existence is built upon an essential self-deception that is transcended by a move to the ethical mode, which is in turn seen to be built upon a more sophisticated version of the same deception, and so must be transcended by a move to the religious mode. But such a claim effectively violates one of his own specifications of the nature of existence spheres. For to present them as offering progressively more adequate answers to a single question amounts to claiming that a correct application of the understanding will reveal that the successive transitions from one sphere to the next and their termination in the sphere of the religious are demanded by reason, that logic alone compels this movement. But to say that a given mode of life is a real existential possibility is to say that it has enough internal coherence to maintain itself, or more precisely to allow that an individual may find it both rationally and spiritually satisfying to continue to live her life in its terms; judgements of relative superiority can and will of course be made, but they will be made by existing individuals, and so from the perspective of one mode of existence rather than another, employing the vocabulary and standards natural to that mode. Such judgements therefore cannot be held to have objective universal authority over all individuals no matter what sphere they occupy; indeed, to do so would be to imagine that existing individuals might inhabit a perspective outside existence, and would thus amount to transforming an essentially subjective question (What is my relation to this possible mode of existence?) into an objective one (Which of these possible modes of existence, impersonally speaking, is the most adequate?).

Moreover, the passages in which Climacus develops his argument for the objective rational superiority of the religious existence sphere over its competitors are shot through with further signs of inappropriate objectivity. For he presents that argument as one that has been developed in a contemporary series of pseudonymous texts written by Soren Kierkegaard: each such text is seen as elucidating one or more existence spheres, and as forming one step in a broader argumentative sweep composed by the pseudonymous authorship as a whole (he assumes 'as is commonly done, that the pseudonymous books are by one author'[10]). But in so presenting them, Climacus at once fails to respect the integrity and specificity of each pseudonym (regarding everything each one of them says as Kierkegaard's opinion or at least as subordinate to Kierkegaard's argumentative purpose) and the integrity and specificity of their texts (taking their careful delineations of concrete individuals in specific relations and situations and filleting them, transforming them into avocations of easily summarisable theses).

To cap it all, Climacus presents these texts as performing a task that he set himself to execute after overhearing an affecting scene between an old man and his grandchild at the graveside of the child's father, when the grandfather extorts an oath from his uncomprehending charge to avoid the philosophical distractions from faith that led the child's father to a godless death. But the fact that someone else could do everything that Climacus then set himself to do, and that he had thought of as the discovery of what would give meaning to his life, suggests that he has a weak grasp upon what it is for one's life to have meaning. For of course what is required for the carrying out of such a project is a talent that others may have, and that Climacus himself might not have had; in other words, the project's significance depends upon certain, essentially contingent facts about him, and to think that such facts might confer significance on his life as a whole is to adopt an essentially aesthetic attitude to life – the most inadequate such attitude by Climacus' own lights. Moreover, the project is an essentially philosophical one: it amounts to developing arguments designed to remind people of the objective superiority of Christianity. And this is the lesson Climacus draws from the lengths to which the grandfather is driven in order to prevent his grandson from being infected by philosophical temptations! It's enough to make one think that Climacus himself has been too much infected by philosophy to be wholly trustworthy.

I think that this judgement cannot in the end be gainsaid: but in order to appreciate its proper significance, we need to remember that every error that Climacus' text embodies is one against which he explic-

itly warns us. Climacus himself points out that the
Christian 'cannot believe nonsense against the understanding ... because the understanding will penetrat-
ingly perceive that it is nonsense and hinder him in
believing it'.[11] He declares that the idea of an 'imma-
nent transition [between existence spheres] is ... a
chimera, a fancy, as if the one standpoint on its own
necessarily determined its transition over to another,
since the category of transition is itself a break in
immanence, is a *leap*'.[12] In the course of offering his
capsule summaries of the other pseudonymous texts,
he castigates a reviewer of his own earlier work for
reporting its contents – 'the report is didactic, purely
and simply didactic; consequently the reader will re-
ceive the impression that the pamphlet is also didactic.
As I see it, this is the most mistaken impression one
can have of it.'[13] And, perhaps most importantly of all,
after spending several hundred pages developing sophisticated philosophical arguments seemingly designed to demonstrate the truth of his opinion that
Christianity fits perfectly with the passionately contradictory nature of human existence, he appends a
section entitled 'An Understanding with the Reader' in
which he declares that the book is 'superfluous', that
he has 'no opinions' about the topics it discusses, that
'anyone who appeals to it has *eo ipso* misunderstood it'
and that this concluding section should be understood
as a complete 'revocation of the book'.

It seems, then, that Climacus is someone who is
intellectually clear-sighted enough to be well aware of
the erroneous nature of every mistake he makes, but
who persists in making them. How are we, his readers,
to relate to this fact about him? How are we to understand his succumbing to the very temptations he diagnoses? The first thing we must recall is that he is not

a Christian, but he is a philosopher; he explicitly denies that religion has a foothold in his life, and his hostility to speculative philosophy does not guarantee that his own standpoint is non-philosophical. On the contrary: his misplaced reaction to the graveyard scene underlines what his biography (*De Omnibus Dubitandum Est*[14]) took pains to stress – that, despite his intellectual recognition of the spiritual dangers to which philosophy opens us up, he is none the less continually tempted to act like a philosopher. And it is this conflict within him that the progress of the *Postscript* enacts. We began with him emphasising that the concepts of belief, evidence and certainty do not function in religious contexts in the way that they function in empirical contexts – that a disinterested rational approach to religious beliefs amounts to a misunderstanding of their true nature. This point was then developed into the wider claim that philosophy's tendency to focus upon the objective aspect of truth repressed its subjective aspect, and so tended to hide the point that ethical teachings were designed to articulate a mode of life, an existential possibility with respect to which individuals must decide whether or not to actualize it, to enact its demands. So far, so good: but then we found ourselves being offered, not just an elucidation of the Christian existence-possibility, but an attempted rational demonstration of its superiority. In other words, despite knowing that adopting the objective, impersonal form of a philosophical argument essentially betrays the point that he was initially concerned to make, Climacus none the less ends by adopting it.

The argument designed to move us through the various existence-spheres by dint of pure reason is the most egregious form of this error; for this amounts to presenting the famous leap of faith, the sort of spiritual

commitment which Climacus begins by sharply distin-
guishing from that which can be supported by the
exercise of disinterested reason, as none the less following automatically upon the provision of a rational
argument or a conceptual account. It may seem that
the argument emphasizing the absolute absurdity of
Christianity avoids this mistake, because it presents
Christianity's capacity to *repel* reason as the basis of
its claim to superiority. But in fact it demonstrates
exactly the same internal incoherence, for reason is
required to appreciate this point; the essential irrelevance to faith of objective, disinterested reason is presented as an insight that only objective reason can
vouchsafe to us, a truth that can only be perceived with
the aid of a new philosophical apparatus or theory.

This, one might say, is the last philosophical temptation – the final, most tenacious form of the error that
Climacus is attempting to extirpate, the error of transforming an existential challenge into an intellectual
problem. For the basic point he wishes to make about
Christianity at the outset is that the challenge it poses
to the individual is an existential one, one whose difficulty lies in the demand it places on us to live a very
specific and very challenging form of life; but his own
response to that insight is ultimately to transform the
challenge into an intellectual one – as if, without
developing and deploying certain conceptions of truth,
existence and paradox, the question of how to become
a Christian cannot be properly understood or con-
fronted. But the task at hand is to *live* in a certain way,
and for that task no special application of the intellect
is needed (the Gospels make it very clear what a
Christian life requires), and neither is any special
array of intellectual skills (the difference between the
peasant and the wise man, Climacus tells us, is that

the former knows what the latter must come to know that he knows). What is needed is rather a special application (or re-orientation of the will;) and, by his example, Climacus shows us that what is needed by philosophers is a re-orientation of their will to knowledge, of their compulsive tendency to think that all problems are intellectual problems. They must give up the impulse to think that philosophical knowledge is an essential preliminary to faith, even in the essentially self-abnegating form in which Climacus himself develops it. To give philosophy even the self-critical role of demonstrating its own essential irrelevance is still to give it a species of relevance – and that is to give it too much.

It therefore seems that the true teaching of the *Postscript* is that one must stop doing philosophy altogether – not just restrict one's philosophizing to attacks on the impulse to philosophize about faith, but stop philosophizing. It means realizing that even the *Postscript*, with its unremitting attack on philosophical pretensions, still retains philosophical pretensions which must be abandoned or revoked. But of course, that is precisely what Climacus tells us to do in the Appendix to the *Postscript* – a piece of advice that he couples with the assertion that 'to write a book and to revoke it is not the same as refraining from writing it'. Why not? Because simply not writing philosophy would necessarily fail to communicate the lesson Climacus has it in mind to teach; but writing a book in which he declares that all philosophizing about faith must stop would be a self-defeating instance of direct communication. The only option is to communicate the lesson indirectly – by presenting a concretely realized existential possibility in which the last, most tenacious form of the error to be extirpated is manifest to us, in a

manner which initially tempts us to identify ourselves
with it but which gradually reveals its absurdity, thus
giving us the chance to recognize the error for what it
is and so to appropriate the truth. In other words,
Climacus offers us all of the indirect evidence we need
to judge for ourselves that the persona he presents to
the reader embodies not the truth but a further version
of the misapprehension to which he is opposed, in the
hope that we can recognize ourselves in him and so go
beyond the perspective he pretends to occupy. This is
the true locus of his irony and humour: as he points
out, to be a humorist is to have 'an uncommon sense
for the comic and a certain talent for making ludicrous
what is ludicrous'.[15] He makes himself the butt of his
own humour, doing his indirect utmost to make the
latent ludicrousness of his project patent to his readers
(the relish with which he invents his give-away account of the graveyard scene that supposedly inspired
him to his philosophical task is almost palpable); and
the best understanding to which he could come with
them would be one in which they find him as comic in
his own way as the Hegelian speculative philosophers
he so persistently lampoons, and so find the strength
to extirpate every vestige of the ludicrousness that
infects their own existence as philosophers.

4

The Transcendence of Self

It may seem that commencing a further chapter in a work on the philosophy of religion after the conclusion of the previous one indicates a failure on my part to transform that intellectual insight into practical action – a reduplication of Climacus' besetting sin. But that sin must be correctly characterised: it takes the form of presuming that philosophy (whether in the form of an argument or a new conceptual apparatus) is an essential prerequisite for faith. And there are some elements of Climacus' endeavour which avoid that presumption rather than exemplifying it; in particular, there is his early elucidation of the logical grammar of the concept of religious belief, and his subsequent stress on the point that summarising ethical teachings in the form of propositions risks obscuring the demand they impose for existential resolution. Both should be thought of as diagnoses of intellectual misapprehensions to which philosophers (and others) are prone, and so as attempts to remove illusory obstacles to perceiving the true challenge posed by religious teachings rather than as attempts to provide a conceptual apparatus without which religious faith is unobtainable. Accordingly, they do not amount to further expressions of the philosophical will to knowledge; and taken together, they imply a possible middle ground for the philosophy of religion – a terrain on which the extreme

strategies of founding faith upon rational demonstration and defining faith as absolutely repellent to reason
might both be avoided.

This strategy of avoidance effectively returns us to
the programme outlined at the end of Chapter Two,
where Climacus' early insights were taken to suggest
that anyone interested in appropriately (i.e. indirectly)
communicating the nature of Christianity must do so
not by providing empirical grounding for belief in a
divine entity but by providing an account of the form
of life Christianity demands from those who claim to
believe in it – to show what the concept of *religious*
belief means by reminding us of the form of life within
which it has a use. The only legitimate task in the
philosophy of religion is, then, to clarify what distinguishes a life in which religion has a place from one in
which it has none, and to clarify what distinguishes
Christianity from its religious competitors. The aim is
to show that, despite philosophical qualms, it is a
possible mode of existence (i.e. it is internally coherent,
embodying a comprehensible attitude to life), but to do
so in a way which makes it clear that it is merely one
possibility among a range of others, in relation to which
each individual is required to make a choice but is not
required to make a particular choice.

From this perspective, much good use can be made
of the material Climacus deploys in the course of his
deliberately confused argumentative strategies. For
example, if we abstract from the evolutionary logic of
his presentation of the aesthetic, ethical and religious
modes of life, then he can be regarded as having iso-
lated the distinctive characteristics of each; and what
distinguishes the religious mode is its attempt to articulate the meaning of life by relating it to something
of absolute value outside the world, i.e. to God. In the

final third of the *Postscript*, Climacus elucidates what that might mean in existential terms in much more detail, under the rubric of a discussion of religiousness 'A'.

He isolates three inter-related factors in that mode of existence, all of which are encapsulated in the slogan: simultaneously to relate oneself absolutely to one's absolute good and relatively to one's relative goods. If God is understood as the absolute good, then in relation to him, all finite, intra-worldly goods are of relative worth; accordingly, those desirous of relating themselves to God must relate themselves to all other goods as relative goods, which means living a life in which they have only relative importance. If, like the aesthete, someone regards the achievement of a certain goal or the satisfaction of a certain desire as solely determinant of the meaning of her life, and so is prepared to sacrifice all other goods for its sake, then her life reveals that she is relating herself absolutely to a relative good and relatively to the absolute good. If, like the ethicist, she regards her capacity for autonomous choice as the sole ground of her life's meaning, and is prepared to sacrifice any other good if it should conflict with the maintenance and exercise of that autonomy (if, like Kant, she holds that divine pronouncements must have their goodness validated by the self-given moral law), then once again her life reveals that she is conferring absolute status on a relative good and relative status on the absolute good. Only if she is prepared to regard any finite good as dispensable when it comes into conflict with the divine will can she be said to be relating absolutely to the absolute good.

In other words, relating absolutely to the absolute good and relatively to relative goods are not two separable components of the religious form of life but rather

two different ways of characterizing it. To relate absolutely to God, to give that relation absolute importance
in one's life, is not something to which we must turn
our attention in addition to attempting to relate relatively to our relative goods; to regard those goods as
having only relative importance, to be prepared to give
them up for God's sake and to regard their continued
possession as a gift from God, just *is* to relate absolutely to the absolute good. As Climacus puts it, the
absolute good is distinctive precisely because 'it can be
defined only by the mode in which it is acquired';[16] the
absolute good just is that which can be acquired only
by being prepared to venture everything, to give everything up for its sake. Money can be defined inde-
pendently of the ways in which it might be acquired,
because it can be acquired in many ways; a relation to
God can only be acquired by being prepared to divest
oneself of any and all other goods, and so is manifest
only in the manifestations of that preparedness. In
other words, the fact that God, as the absolute good,
lies outside the contingent, finite world does not entail
that the nature of any relation to him cannot be given
a full and concrete specification in terms of a relation
to contingency and finitude – the stuff of ordinary
human experience.

Neither is that God-respecting relation to finite
goods one of absolute rejection or renunciation. It is of
course true that those who wish to establish a relation
to God will almost certainly begin from a position of
immersion in finitude, regarding relative goods as of
absolute importance; and as a consequence, they must
practise renouncing those relative goods if they are to
make any space at all in their lives for an absolute
relation to the absolute good. But the ultimate goal of
such penitential rites is not to regard all such goods as

entirely worthless, and any relation to them as a mis-
relation: to do so would be to deny our divinely-created
nature as human beings and the goodness of the created world. The aim is rather to look differently upon
those goods, to re-orient our sense of their worth and
of its source: it is to re-establish a relation to ordinary
goals, desires and needs that reflects their contingency
by assigning only relative importance to them. The
religious believer is thus not someone who avoids the
pleasures of a good meal, companionship or a walk in
the park; her life will be filled with just the ordinary
array of ordinary human activities, but her attitude to
them will be different. To adapt some of Climacus'
examples: she will imaginatively anticipate the de-
lights of the banquet she believes that her husband is
preparing, but will devour the bread and cheese with
which he actually presents her with undimmed joy.
She will resist the impulse to go for a walk insofar as
it appears an expression of self-indulgence, but she will
endorse it insofar as it seems to express a simply
human need for diversion; and aware that the distinction between indulgence and recreation, between self-
ishness and the limitations of finitude, is always
uncertain in the concrete case, she will act as seems
best to her in the knowledge that God will lovingly
acknowledge her humanness just as her actions strive
to acknowledge her humanness to God.

Beyond renunciation and suffering (thus understood), Climacus speaks of guilt as the third mark of
the religious form of life. The ethical attitude demands
that one measure one's life against the moral law, and
such measurements often reveal past failures to live
up to its demands; but the ethicist thinks that such
failures can be gathered up into the self's capacity for
self-governance through repentance. Repentance ac-

knowledges these failures as transgressions but also
as past ones, as specific errors whose taint can be fully
neutralized or eradicated by this acknowledgement
and a successful resolution not to repeat them; it thus
restores the individual to the state of essentially guilt-
less integrity from which she has temporarily fallen
away. From a religious perspective, such an attitude
to transgression is doubly untenable. First, insofar as
we interpret the standard of goodness as the absolute
good (i.e. as God), then even the most minimal particle
of guilt makes us absolutely guilty; one transgression,
however small, removes us absolutely from the goodness to which we are striving to relate ourselves, re-
vealing a possibility in us that is absolutely absent
from God and thus signifying an essential difference
between us and him. Secondly, the revelation of a
transgression through self-examination is not just
likely but inevitable. For the standard in that examination is not just absolute; it also applies to my life as
a whole, and so to every moment of that life. But insofar
as all human existence is a matter of finding oneself in
a present moment facing the responsibilities of the
next, then even if my first moment of awareness of the
good produces an immediate and completely successful
enactment of its demands, that enactment cannot
reach back to include the moment of awareness from
which it began; it cannot redeem its own existential
origins. To become aware of the demands of the good
is not to enact them, but it is to become aware that one
is not at present enacting them; and that failure of
enactment is irredeemable, so no one's enactment of
the good can redeem their lives as a whole. In this
sense, the temporal structure of existence makes us
essentially guilty, depriving us of the capacity to bring
our life as a whole into relation to the good; it ensures

that guilt is not an occasional and aberrant state that leaves the attainability of the ethical ideal of moral perfection unquestioned, but is rather an essential qualification of our nature.

The religious conception of guilt thus characterises human beings and God as absolutely different from one another in moral terms: in relation to God, the eternal and absolute good, human beings are as nothing. Establishing such a relation therefore amounts to acknowledging this absolute difference by acknowledging oneself as nothing – a species of moral self-abnegation. And formulating matters this way allows us to see that the other two marks of the religious attitude also amount to species of self-abnegation – that the relativizing of one's relation to relative goods and the suffering and renunciation thereby experienced should be understood not merely as renunciations of the goods but as renunciations of the self. After all, in renouncing the absolute value we attach in ethical mode to our capacity for autonomous choice, we renounce our will and the ego of which it is the expression; and insofar as that capacity is the hidden source of the value we attach to relative goods in the aesthetic mode, then renouncing those goods amounts to self-renunciation. In dying to immediacy, dying to the world's absolute valuation of its relative goods, one is asked to die to the self.

Such a death is not, however, the end of the self, but rather the negative face of a process of re-birth, of the self being born into a new life. For example, part of a life lived in accordance with such a demand will involve one's relations with others, and so will involve dying to the claims of the self in that context, of losing oneself in the other. The religious believer thinks of any and every other as her neighbour, and she loves her neigh-

bour – but not because of any particular relationship
in which the two stand (as relatives, lovers, friends),
rather simply because the neighbour is there; she is
loved not because of who she is but because she *is*,
because of her sheer contingent existence. Such love
demands the renunciation of those reciprocal claims
that human beings normally and legitimately advance
in the context of a loving relationship with others – the
believer places no limits on her responses to her neighbour's claim on her, does not expect reciprocation or
consideration from her, does not resent ingratitude,
deceit or betrayal. Her love is independent of the way
things go, unchanging and immune from defeat; and
insofar as she achieves this, she loses herself in God by
dying to the claims of the self.

It is striking that, if we look back on the three
defective proofs of God's existence examined earlier in
the light of this elucidation of the nature of a religious
form of life, they can be seen as (malformed) attempts
to articulate analogous points about the logical grammar of religious concepts.[17]

Let us take the ontological argument first. We have
already seen the defects inherent in Anselm's assumption that existence is a perfection; but running in
tandem with an argument based on that assumption
in his texts is another which is based on a superficially
similar but in fact crucially different presupposition.
Its structure is as follows. God is a being than which
nothing greater can be conceived; a being whose non-
existence is logically impossible is greater than a being
whose non-existence is logically possible; therefore
God is a being whose non-existence is logically impossible. The assumption guiding this argument is that
the logical impossibility of non-existence is a perfection, i.e. that it is not existence but necessary existence

that is a perfection; and this assumption avoids the ills
to which its relative is heir.

Many existing things are ones whose non-existence
is logically possible; and this means that they can
properly be called dependent and limited. Dependent,
in that they rely for their existence on other things: my
word-processor was brought into existence through the
efforts of certain persons and machines, and its continued existence is dependent on its not being assaulted
with a crow-bar or dropped on the floor. Such dependence also involves limitation: my word-processor's construction and functioning was and is dependent on a
supply of electricity, and so can be said to be limited by
it. Since such things manifest different degrees of
dependence and limitation, they can be ranked accordingly: a word processor as good as mine that could also
survive being dropped on the floor would be superior
to mine, as would one that did not require electricity.
By contrast, God is a non-dependent and unlimited
being: there are not and could not be any limits to his
powers, and he does not and could not depend on
anything else for coming into or continuing in existence. This is what is meant by claiming that he is a
being than which nothing greater can be conceived; his
superiority just is, in part, his essential freedom from
limitation. But such freedom distinguishes him from
entities of the ordinary sort; and since their dependence and limitation is a reflection of the logical possibility of their non-existence, we must conclude that
God differs from them in that respect as well, i.e. that
his non-existence is not logically possible. He is, in short,
an eternal being, one to whom the qualities associated
with contingent, spatio-temporal existence necessarily
do not apply; it is not even that he endures endlessly, for
it makes sense to say of something that has always

existed and will always exist that it might not have
existed, and that would be to impose a limitation on a
being conceived of as absolutely without limits.

It is for this reason that Anselm's second argument
avoids the Kantian objection that existence is not a real
predicate, i.e. that the question whether a being exists
is settleable only by investigating the world and not by
elucidating a concept. It is undeniable that, if that
question is a genuinely open one, then an empirical
investigation will be needed to settle it; to establish the
truth about my claim that there is a word processor in
my study, you need to look. But Anselm's point is that,
with respect to God, that question simply is not open;
if it were, he would not be a perfect, absolutely unlimited being. To believe that, in establishing that God's
existence is necessary, Anselm has merely established
that if God exists then he necessarily exists, is to take
back with the antecedent what is given with the con-
sequent; it is to make God's necessary existence contingent. On the other hand, Anselm's argument does
not demonstrate the rational necessity of belief in God:
it highlights the point that any being a greater than
which cannot be conceived is one whose existence cannot be thought of as contingent. This means that his
existence is either logically necessary or logically impossible (i.e. that the concept is either self-contradic-
tory or nonsensical) – which leaves open the possibility
that someone will fail to find any sense in the idea of
religious belief or see any point in the form of a religious life. But it does exclude the possibility of rejecting
such a life on the grounds that it embodies a dubious
or false hypothesis – for if Anselm's argument is right,
it definitively excludes the idea that God's existence is
a question of fact, settleable by employing the usual
empirical investigative methods.

This second, recessive strand in the ontological argument thus stresses the fundamental insight from which Climacus' whole understanding of the nature of religious belief flows, for it demonstrates that a belief in God is not a species of empirical belief, and so that God is not an entity of the sort with which we are familiar, a denizen of space and time, but something absolutely different. As we saw earlier, however, it does not follow from this that establishing a God-relation, directing one's attention to a being understood as beyond space and time, involves directing one's attention away from the finite world entirely; it means rather reorienting one's relation to that world and to the world's assessment of the value of the goods it offers – it means dying to the self. And the cosmological argument can be interpreted as a (malformed) attempt to articulate just that insight.

That argument offers a view of God as first cause, as an answer to the question why there is something rather than nothing when that is understood as a request for a causal explanation. The flaws in the argument derived from its assumption that a causal explanation might intelligibly be given of the existence of the world as a whole – as if the world were an unusually big object and God an unusually powerful and extra-worldly entity. However, to say that that assumption is incoherent is to reject one sort of answer to this question, and so one interpretation of that question; it is not to reject the question *in toto*. For when we ask why there is anything at all, we need not be asking for the details of any causal process or development; we may rather be concerned about the sense, meaning or reality of everything (as opposed to something in particular). We may, in other words, have been led to ask why there is something rather than nothing because we have been struck by the sheer contingent existence of the world – not how it is, but that it is – and so have been led to ponder what, if anything, its existence (and ours within it) might signify. The riddle thus posed cannot of course be answered by reference to any facts within the world or by illegitimately attempting to explain the 'fact' of the world's existence as if it were a fact within the world; and invoking God as if his existence were a fact outside the world will be no improvement. But to identify as divine a perspective which is capable of taking in the world as a whole, from which alone it is possible to relate to the world as a whole, may well provide the beginnnings of an answer – if we understand our relation to that perspective in terms of a striving to relate to the world in a way which thoroughly respects its thorough-going contingency by relativizing our relation to each and every thing in that world.

An individual who thirsts for money relativizes her relation to other finite goods, regarding their worth as limited in comparison with money and so turning away from that part of her world; but she simultaneously absolutizes her relation to money and so anchors herself within the world as a whole, adopting an intra-worldly perspective. Someone who is concerned for the moral law will not worry if she loses the money that an immoral action would have brought her, but she will still have certain moral expectations, regarding herself as possessed of rights that others should respect and feeling harmed and deserving of recompense if they are neglected; she thus continues to be concerned about how the world treats her, and so remains anchored to an intra-worldly perspective. The religious believer attempts to see the world from the point of view of the eternal, and so strives to renounce even the expecta-

tions created by moral rights; and insofar as she suc-
ceeds, the relative significance she attaches to intra-
worldly matters precisely corresponds to their
contingency, and so renders her untouched alike by
their existence or their disappearance, by all the vicis-
situdes to which (as the ontological argument makes
clear) their limited and dependent nature inevitably
makes them vulnerable. From her perspective, therefore, each thing within the world is seen as if the world
as a whole were its backdrop and so as part of a sheerly
contingent whole; how the world goes is thereby reduced to vanishing point in comparison with the 'fact'
of its sheerly contingent existence. In short, the religious believer attains a perspective on the world as a
whole by dying to the attributions of significance that
are secreted by every perspective within it; but to do so
is to go beyond any concern for how the world treats
her, and so amounts to dying to the self.

Since the argument from design specifically focusses
upon how the world is rather than that it is, it may
seem immune to the restorative re-interpretation just
outlined for its cosmological relative. But if we retain
our understanding of the religious perspective as cen-
tred on a practice of dying to the self, then we can
reinterpret this argument's initial stress upon the order and beauty of the world in terms which relate it
immediately to that form of life. Here, some words of
Simone Weil are relevant:

> The beautiful: that which we do not want to
> change. The good: not to want to change it, in fact
> (non-intervention). The true: not to want to
> change it in one's mind (by means of illusion).[18]

Edifying tracts have often linked truth, beauty and

goodness; here we see one possible reason for so doing. Weil's claim is that the natural human response to the perception of the true underlying order of the world and to its evident beauties is umbilically linked to an essential aspect of the religious understanding of the good, namely the transcendence of self. To value truth is to desire a picture of reality that is unclouded by the flaws of one's subjectivity, its desires and fantasies; to value beauty is to see in the beautiful object something that ought to be preserved, and in particular from the ego's desire to consume what it encounters – to make use of it as a means to its ends. In both cases, our attention is caught and held by that which is not the self; our experience of the beautiful and of the true thus directs our concerns outward and away from our desires and our will, as if preparing us for (and in part introducing us to) the religious practice of dying to the self by achieving a perspective from which we are unmoved by – and so bereft of any desire to interfere with – how the world goes. That a subliminal awareness of the links between these modes of selflessness should have been channelled into the form of an argument from design may be regrettable; but it is hardly surprising, and it should not prevent us from seeing the edificatory aspect of human responses to the beauty of the natural order.

A similarly edificatory lesson can be drawn from attention to those aspects of the natural order which have led philosophers and religious believers to talk of the problem of evil. To respond to suffering in one's own life that is brought about by natural causes rather than human intervention (e.g. the painful illness and death of one's child) by hypothesising that it is the means to a greater good (either for oneself or for the human race) is to transform the God who is imagined to bring it about into a moral criminal. It amounts to responding to that suffering by asking 'Why is this happening to me?' – as if one's rights (at the very least, one's right to a non-natural explanation) had been violated; and that amounts to placing weight on the self and its demands. But such suffering can also be used to teach us the contrary lesson, namely that the self is nothing; the very fact that it seems undeserved, and so seems to violate our sense of what is due to us as moral beings, can help us to see that nothing is due to us – that we are not the centre of the universe or of any 'moral' blueprint for its development. Experiencing evil can thus be seen as a challenge to accept that how the world goes is irrelevant, that one must transcend any concern for how the world goes by dying to the self's imperious demands – whether for preservation, for recompense, or even for explanation.

Of course, it is not open to us to offer the suffering of others to God in this way; if, for the religious believer, evil is elevation of self and goodness is its negation, then (as we saw earlier) goodness demands that one die to one's own rights and demands in the context of relations with others – and that means striving to sacrifice oneself to others, offering unstinting help to them in their misfortunes rather than making use of them by merely contemplating their misfortunes as part of a supposedly religious meditation. The point is rather that an essential part of the practice of dying to a concern for self (in one's own life and in one's relations to others) is that of transcending the desire to unearth a justification or explanation for suffering (whether one's own or that of others). Coming to accept that 'the rain falls on the just and the unjust alike' does not require passivity in the face of others' misfortunes, but it does require transcending the demand for a non-natural explanation of (and so for any supernatural justification for) them.

The Originality of Sin

So much for religiousness 'A': but as Climacus never tires of telling us, Christianity – or religiousness 'B' – is an entirely distinct mode of existence, and we have as yet offered nothing to elucidate the difference between a belief in God and a belief in Christ as the Son of God. What we do know is that the terms in which Climacus made this distinction cannot be taken at face value. If we cannot intelligibly talk of degrees or classes of nonsensicality, then Christianity cannot be said to differ from other forms of religious belief by intensifying or rendering absolute the simple paradoxicality or absurdity inherent in the religious demand that finite individuals relate themselves to the eternal. We can, however, take guidance from the way in which Climacus explained *how* Christianity renders that paradoxicality absolute. For, according to the *Postscript*, it does so by offering its followers a conception of the eternal which is itself paradoxical, thus ensuring that the object of Christian faith, as well as the relation in which individuals stand towards it, is inherently paradoxical. In other words, Climacus' talk of absolute paradoxicality highlights the doctrine of the Incarnation, of God becoming man; it implies that the distinctiveness of Christianity flows from its teaching that believers can and must take up their paradoxical relation to the eternal by relating themselves to a particular, historical, fully human individual.

Much follows from this: enough, in fact, to form the basis of one possible understanding of the Christian form of life. For on Climacus' account, although Christianity clearly resembles other religions in its imposition of the paradoxical demand that individuals relate to the eternal, it may be thought to make that relation more humanly comprehensible in a certain sense; for it conceives of the eternal not as something entirely alien to and separated from the finite world but as having fully taken on its nature, as having become accessible to the individual in the form of another individual. This point is reinforced if we follow Climacus in understanding the general paradoxicality of the God-relation in terms of a requirement to die to the self, to adopt an essentially self-sacrificial form of life; for then his subsequent claim that the object of Christian faith is paradoxical implies that the inner nature of the incarnate Deity is similarly self-sacrificial. In other words, it implies that the Christian God is a God of renunciation and suffering, one whose very nature is to sacrifice himself for others; and it follows from this that, on the Christian conception, self-sacrifice is not just something imposed upon believers by their attempt to relate to God, not just a further regrettable reflection of the infinite difference between their finite nature and that of eternity, but an imitation of the divine nature – a form of life that is a sharing in the divine life.

Our re-interpretation of the 'problem' of evil can be understood to contain just such an edifying lesson.[19] For that 'problem' is structured as follows: if evil exists, then God is either not omniscient and omnipotent or not all-loving. For Christianity, the problem with this 'problem' is that it treats divine omnipotence and divine love as two separate attributes, the one to do with God's capacities and the other with his motivation. What the existence of evil reveals is that they are not separate attributes at all: the Christian God is a God whose only omnipotence is that of love. His creation of the world was not a feat of extreme natural power, but an expression of self-emptying love; it is a ceding of his own power to make way for that of nature and that of human beings, a continual negation of himself in order to facilitate and maintain the existence of the world and of us within it. And of course, this is precisely the sort of love to which Christ's life gives perfect expression – not just in the final, redemptive self-emptying on the cross (a Passion in which God's Son comes to feel forsaken by his Father, experiencing the ultimate affliction), and not just in the ideal of serving others that finds expression in such specific acts as the washing of the disciples' feet, but in the extremity of divine self-abasement that is the act of incarnation itself, in the sheerly paradoxical fact of the divine voluntarily taking on fully human nature. The Resurrection may reveal the glory of existence in God's presence that awaits beyond the bounds of finitude; but the essentially self-sacrificial nature of the God-man's life on earth, the fact that it took the form of unremitting renunciation and suffering unto death, shows that a human life spent striving to give expression to the love of God on earth will demand a continuous dying to the self.

This, in part, is what Christ claims when he says that 'I am the way, the truth and the life': His life is the Christian form of life, and insofar as believers succeed in actualizing it, they enact a bodying forth of the divine life on earth – an overcoming rather than a

further expression of the distance between finitude
and the eternal. But Christ also claims to be the way
and the truth: and Climacus understands this to mean
that anyone wishing to establish a relation to the truth,
Christianly understood, must establish a personal relation with Christ. In part, this means that the Christian God is one with whom a personal relation is
possible: the eternal is understood not as something
Platonically impersonal, and not as relating primarily
to particular tribes or races, but as relating to specific
individuals. In part, it means that the central moral
source in the Christian life is a concrete, historical
individual; the claim is that establishing an immediate
relation with the God-man (whether in personal experience, or through scripture, or through the Church
and its sacramental ministry) gives an individual access to a source of spiritual energy, contact with which
empowers her to do and be good. Most importantly,
however, it means that in the absence of Christ's incarnation, we could not have had full or proper access to
the truth; and this implies that a personal relation to
Christ is not only possible but also necessary to our
spiritual well-being – in effect, that Christ's coming
was an essential prerequisite for human beings to be
capable of relating to the good at all.

The crucial point here is that Christ does not merely
possess the truth – he *is* the truth. To be sure, his
teachings on moral and spiritual matters as recorded
in Scripture and transmitted through the Church are
central to his purpose, defining the form of life to which
his followers must aspire; but their authority, their
compelling claim upon our attention, is understood by
Christians to rest upon the fully divine nature of the
one teaching them. Prophets may speak the word of
God, but that is because God is speaking through them;

Jesus is God

Christ speaks the word of God because he *is* the Word of God.

The consequences of this point can be most clearly seen if we use the terms provided by our earlier discussion of subjective and objective truth. If the Christian truth were simply a message Christ brought to us, then its content would be essentially detachable from his person, and his coming to bring it would be of vanishing importance – merely one way of conveying to us a message that we would in principle be capable of grasping in his absence. But for the Christian, the truth is the person of Christ, so his coming is of absolutely decisive significance; without it we would not merely have remained ignorant of something that we were none the less perfectly capable of grasping, we would also have lacked that essential capacity or condition for understanding. But if Christ's coming into existence simultaneously brings us the truth and the condition for understanding that truth, it follows that in the absence of his coming, we are outside the truth, not just ignorant of it but essentially oriented away from it. Since, however, the capacity to seek and understand truth is what distinguishes us from other animals, we humans cannot have been created lacking that capacity, but must rather have been deprived of it; and since God would not have so deprived us, and no contingent happening could have deprived us of an essential qualification of our nature, we must have brought about that deprivation ourselves. In short, if the Incarnation is to have the decisive significance Christians attribute to it, human beings must be seen as not merely lacking the truth and not merely existing as untruth, but as having removed themselves from the condition of truth to that of untruth – as having forfeited the truth through an essentially truth-hating impulse of their own nature.

This is the Christian concept of the originally sinful nature of human beings; and, by deepening and transcending the concept of guilt, it most fundamentally distinguishes Christian religious belief from the various forms of religiousness 'A'. Understanding human existence in terms of guilt involves thinking of individuals as always and essentially in the wrong in relation to the absolute good; but it preserves the idea that recognizing the need for, and actually establishing, such a relation to the good is always possible, and equally possible for every individual. The concept of (original) sin entails that human beings must be understood as having forfeited the possibility of establishing such a relation by their own action, because they have enslaved themselves to untruth; they have freely bound their will to it, and so have simultaneously rendered themselves unable to will a re-orientation of that will and incapable of conceiving of their present condition as one in which they are essentially deprived of the truth. Their salvation therefore depends upon the intervention of Christ, who must gratuitously will to incarnate himself and to establish a personal relation with a given individual (since she is unable to establish it for herself), and thereby simultaneously introduce a new conception of herself as sinful, a re-orientation of her will towards the truth and a direct encounter with it. But this salvation, dependent as it is upon a relation with a concrete, historical individual, is not equally open to all; any fully historical phenomenon is locked in time and space, so any individual's access to it is determined by its temporal location relative to her.

As one might expect, this difference can be articu-

lated in terms of selfhood and self-relation. Understanding one's existence in terms of guilt changes an
individual by changing her sense of her status in relation to the good, but that same relation to the absolute
also confers unity on her life as a whole, giving her a
self whose integrity cannot be shipwrecked by contingency; in that sense, establishing a God-relation
amounts to a re-birth of the self from the threat and
reality of dispersal in finitude. Understanding one's
existence in terms of sin means understanding that
one's coming into existence is a coming into existence
as a sinner; created for eternity as a being possessed of
a capacity to relate to the truth, the individual is born
as a sinner, and so suffers a break in the essential
integrity of her nature, as if her birth is re-birth as a
person other than she was. But the capacity to perceive
one's existence in such terms can be acquired only
through a relation to Christ which simultaneously
permits the possibility of a re-orientation towards the
truth, and thus a reintegration of one's fallen nature,
a second re-birth. In short, the absolutely despairing
recognition of oneself as an individual mired in untruth
and the absolutely joyful recognition of oneself as an
individual restored to a relation to the truth are two
sides of the same coin.

Of course, in the absence of a relation to Christ, the
Christian conception of human existence will appear
absolutely offensive – whether from an ethical or a
non-Christian religious perspective. The idea that the
mere fact of coming into existence might strip individuals of their capacity to relate to the truth and blind
them to that deprivation in a way for which they must
hold themselves responsible, and that the restoration
of that capacity (and so of access to eternal happiness)
is essentially subject to contingency, clearly offends

against central canons of morality and justice – indeed, against some of the most fundamental aspects of our conception of ourselves. To adopt a Christian understanding of self and world will thus inevitably appear to involve rejecting everything that makes us what we are, and so to be no more than a particularly virulent form of self-hatred. But from the perspective of one who has received the gift of Christian faith, that sense of offence – however understandable – is simply a further expression of the truth-hating orientation of the unreconstructed human will and so a further confirmation of human sinfulness. Only the contradictory experience of an extremity of despair over oneself and an extremity of joyful rescue that is the harbinger and heart of an encounter with Christ can overcome that offence; only when life somehow forces us into a position from which Christian concepts appear as the only possible way of accommodating and making sense of our existence can the prospect of a form of life founded on the imitation of Christ elicit our passionate commitment.

*

And what of philosophy in all this? In what sense can this and the preceding chapter be thought of as philosophical investigations, as opposed to poor attempts at edification or the unwitting provision of ample grounds for taking offence? Is there really room here for an exercise of reason that is not an employment of it on one side or another of the existential choice with which Christianity faces us?

Only if the following distinction can be made and observed: the distinction between a description and a defence of (or an attack upon) a form of life. For what can then follow is a distribution of duties, a division of intellectual labour. On this understanding, philosophy can spell out the central features of the forms of life that face one another across the divide between religious and other modes of human existence, and bring us to see how each will inevitably appear to the other. It can help to remove misunderstandings and other intellectual obstacles that might stand between an individual and a well-founded decision about the challenge religion poses to her way of life. It can even elucidate the types of intelligible and pertinent consideration that are likely to be brought to bear by contending parties should anyone attempt to argue in favour of a particular decision on this matter, and so demonstrate that such choices are not bereft of, or beyond, rationality. But it neither can, nor should, attempt to engage in those arguments with, let alone to make that choice for, its readers. The latter is always an error; the former is the business of edification, engagement, substantive discussion. It is, of course, neither an intellectually nor an ethically illegitimate enterprise – it is a perfectly valid use to which human reason might be put, and forms a central part of any individual's life; but it is not a philosophical use of reason, and it should form no part of a philosopher's life *qua* philosopher. A philosopher should never forget that she is a human being, but not everything that a human being may do should be done in philosophy's name. As Climacus might say, philosophy is not an edifying business.[20]

Notes

1. I. Kant, *Groundwork of the Metaphysic of Morals*, in H. Paton (ed.), *The Moral Law* (Hutchinson, London: 1948), p. 73.

2. B. Pascal, *Pensées*, trans. A.J. Krailsheimer (Penguin, London: 1966), p. 169.

3. Much of the argumentative material to follow is derived from Norman Malcolm's essay 'Anselm's Ontological Arguments' (in *Philosophical Review LXIX*, 1960), and from the work of D.Z. Phillips – in particular, the essays 'Hume's Legacy' (in *Religion Without Explanation* [Blackwell, Oxford: 1976]) and 'From World to God?' (in *Faith and Philosophical Enquiry* [Routledge, London: 1970]), and Chapter Five of *The Concept of Prayer* (Blackwell, Oxford: 1965).

4. H. McCabe, *God Matters* (Chapman, London: 1987), ch. 1.

5. F. Dostoevsky, *The Brothers Karamazov*, trans. C. Garnett (Everyman, London: 1950), p. 250.

6. The pseudonym employed by Soren Kierkegaard in those of his writings which most directly concern the relation between philosophy and faith, namely: *Philosophical Fragments* (Princeton University Press, Princeton N.J.: 1985), and *Concluding Unscientific Postscript to the Philosophical Fragments* (Princeton University Press, Princeton N.J.: 1992), both translated by H.V. and E.H. Hong.

7. My argument in this chapter is extensively indebted to the work of James Conant – particularly 'Must We show What We Cannot Say?' (in R. Fleming and M. Payne [eds], *The Senses of Stanley Cavell* [Bucknell University Press, Lewisburg: 1989]), and 'Kierkegaard, Wittgenstein and Nonsense' (in T. Cohen and P. Guyer [eds], *Pursuits of Reason: Essays in Honour of Stanley Cavell*, 1993). Since, however, I venture to extend, elaborate and adapt Conant's own reading of Climacus' authorial strategy in various ways, it should be emphasised that he bears no responsibility for my particular formulations, or any errors and extravagance that may have resulted from them.

8. This interpretation of the first line of argument draws heavily

upon Michael Weston's essay 'Philosophy and Religion in the Thought of Kierkegaard' (in M. McGhee [ed.], *Philosophy, Religion and the Spiritual Life* [Cambridge University Press, Cambridge: 1992), and his book *Kierkegaard and Modern Continental Philosophy* (Routledge, 1994).

9. *Concluding Unscientific Postscript*, p. 230.

10. Ibid., p. 284.

11. Ibid., p. 568.

12. Ibid., p. 295.

13. Ibid., p. 275.

14. An early manuscript now published in the same volume as the *Philosophical Fragments*.

15. *Concluding Unscientific Postscript*, p. 622.

16. Ibid., p. 427.

17. Once again, this re-interpretation of the traditional proofs draws heavily upon the work of Norman Malcolm and D.Z. Phillips, cited in note 1 above.

18. Simone Weil, *Notebooks*, trans. A. Wills (Routledge, London: 1956), vol. I, p.38.

19. Cf. ch. 6 of D.Z. Phillips, *R.S. Thomas: Poet of the Hidden God* (Macmillan, London: 1986).

20. I would like to thank the following for their comments on earlier drafts of these chapters: Jay Bernstein, Stephen Grover, Peter Hacker, John Hyman, Paul Johnston, Michael Weston and Philip Wheatley.

Bibliography

J. Conant, 'Must We Show What We Cannot Say?' in R. Fleming and M. Payne (eds), *The Senses of Stanley Cavell* (Bucknell University Press, Lewisburg: 1989).

J. Conant, 'Wittgenstein, Kierkegaard and Nonsense' in T. Cohen and P. Guyer (eds), *Pursuits of Reason: Essays in Honour of Stanley Cavell* (1993).

F. Dostoevsky, *The Brothers Karamazov*, trans. C. Garnett (Everyman, London: 1950).

I. Kant, *Groundwork of the Metaphysic of Morals* in H. Paton (ed.), *The Moral Law* (Hutchinson, London: 1948).

S. Kierkegaard, *Philosophical Fragments*, trans. H.V. and E.H. Hong (Princeton University Press, Princeton N.J.: 1985).

S. Kierkegaard, *Concluding Unscientific Postscript*, trans. H.V. and E.H. Hong (Princeton University Press, Princeton N.J.: 1992).

H. McCabe, *God Matters* (Chapman, London: 1987).

N. Malcolm, 'Anselm's Ontological Arguments' in *Philosophical Review* LXIX, 1960.

B. Pascal, *Pensées*, trans. A.J. Krailsheimer (Penguin, London: 1966).

D.Z. Phillips, *The Concept of Prayer* (Blackwell, Oxford: 1965).

D.Z. Phillips, *Faith and Philosophical Enquiry* (Blackwell, Oxford: 1970).

D.Z. Phillips, *Religion Without Explanation* (Blackwell, Oxford: 1976).

D.Z. Phillips, *R.S. Thomas: Poet of the Hidden God* (Macmillan, London: 1986).

S. Weil, *Notebooks*, trans. A. Wills (Routledge, London: 1956).

M. Weston, 'Philosophy and Religion in the Thought of Kierkegaard' in M. McGhee (ed.), *Philosophy, Religion and the Spiritual Life* (Cambridge University Press, Cambridge: 1992).

M. Weston, *Kierkegaard and Modern Continental Philosophy* (Routledge, London: 1994).

Index

BEHAVIORISM

John Staddon

James B. Duke Professor of Psychology at Duke
University, North Carolina

Behaviorism was the dominant movement in American psychology in the first half of the twentieth century, culminating in the radical movement of B.F. Skinner, the most influential psychologist since Freud. Skinner wrote at length on social engineering, and his views have influenced all psychologists, both behaviorists and others. Recent developments in theory, robotics and artificial intelligence promise to propel behaviorism once more to the forefront of psychology.

In this entertaining book, John Staddon describes the history of the movement from its beginnings in a short polemic by J.R. Watson in 1913, through the US 'rat runners' to exciting modern developments. He argues that the new theoretical behaviorism can tackle even such problems as 'consciousness', hitherto regarded as the exclusive province of cognitive psychology.

ISBN 0 7156 2488 1

Duckworth, The Old Piano Factory, 48 Hoxton
Square, London N1 6PB
Tel (071) 729 5986, Fax (071) 729 0015

FACTS

Bede Rundle

Fellow of Trinity College, Oxford

Facts have many contrasts: with fiction and fantasy, with speculation and opinion, with hypothesis and theory. Two contrasts of particular interest – to philosophy, to morality, to the natural and social sciences – are those of fact with theory and fact with value, and a central concern of this book is to examine arguments which would have us enlarge these domains at the expense of the realm of facts.

It is naturally supposed either that facts enjoy a concrete existence, being numbered among such worldly items as events, or that they possess a more abstract character, having their home in language. Both alternatives are the source of difficulties, encouraging sceptical claims that the existence of facts is unknowable and their nature impenetrable. An analysis of *fact* is offered which, in rejecting both possibilities, seeks to remove the mystery which surrounds this key concept.

ISBN 0 7156 2467 9

also available in the Interpretations series

LAWS OF NATURE

Rom Harré

Fellow of Linacre College, Oxford

The laws of nature, on which all science is based, are supposed to have three characteristics: to be supported by evidence, to be universally applicable, and to enable us to predict what will always happen in the same circumstances. In this book a philosopher of science examines some of the well-known laws of nature from the point of view of all three characteristics. He shows that science is possible only within a metaphysical framework, a general assumption of the existence of natural kinds. The idea is used to explicate the scope and modality of laws of nature and also to resolve some of the classical paradoxes which have emerged when they are studied in the light of their logical form alone.

ISBN 0 7156 2464 4

also available in the Interpretations series

PARADOXES

Justin Leiber

Professor of Philosophy at the University of
Houston, Texas

Paradoxes are many things. Artificial intelligence views them as viruses of the brain, strange replicators that unexpectedly exploit design possibilities. For the child, they are intellectual cartwheels, an everyday delight. For mathematicians and logicians, they reveal skeletons in the closet of reason. For philosophers and dramatists, they capture the contradictions of experience. The historian of ideas sees that they come in successive waves, surging through Classical Greece, the Renaissance and the twentieth century.

Professor Leiber's user-friendly guide to paradoxes provides an up-to- date survey of an ancient and perennial source of puzzlement.

ISBN 0 7156 2426 1

UNDERSTANDING RELIGION

Eric J. Sharpe

Professor of Religious Studies, University of Sydney

Eric Sharpe's acclaimed work clears the ground for students who are setting out to understand, rather than just to practise, religion.

Understanding Religion discusses, among other things, the relationship between commitment to a particular tradition and the quest for intellectual understanding 'in the round'; 'holiness' as an identifying aspect of religion; functional 'modes' of religion; and finally the question of secularisation.

Assuming throughout that theology and religious studies ought not to be seen as competing approaches, but as sources of complementary insights, it offers the student a fundamental introduction to an important area of enquiry.

'Admirably fitted for its role. Its easy handling of scholarship will be welcomed by those coming to the subject for the first time, yet there is no avoiding the clear message that the study of religion is a serious academic matter.' *The Churchman*

'Theologians and non-theologians alike can learn from this book.' *Journal of Theological Studies*

'To be recommended to both students and teachers.' *Expository Times*

ISBN 0 7156 1735 4

COMPARATIVE RELIGION

A History

Eric J. Sharpe

Professor of Religious Studies, University of Sydney

Described as 'a masterly survey' by the *Times Higher Educational Supplement*, this book is now firmly established as the standard work on the subject.

Eric Sharpe traces the history of comparative religion in detail, from its beginnings in the nineteenth century, in the work of scholars such as Max Muller and anthropologists like Tylor, Lang, Robertson-Smith and Frazer, through the American psychologists of religion (Starbuck, Leuba, William James), to the period after the First World War, when the evolutionary approach was seriously called into question.

Also considered are the relevance to religion of Freud and Jung, the 'phenomenology of religion', the tensions between comparative religion and theology, and the work of such outstanding personalities as Nathan Söderblom and Rudolf Otto. The book's final two chapters review the main issues raised in the subject since the Second World War.

The second edition of this classic work is now available in paperback.

ISBN 0 7156 1081 3

THE APOSTOLIC AGE

G.B. Caird

'A useful and well-documented account of the Apostolic age which reveals sound judgment and a wide acquaintance with the relevant literature.'

British Book News

'An admirable book for all New Testament students, and there is nothing so good or so cheap anywhere else available.' *Methodist Recorder*

'At once an excellent text book and a book of interest and profit for the general reader.' *Expository Times*

'An event of some importance, especially to teachers and students.' *Theology*

ISBN 0 7156 1680 3

THE LANGUAGE AND IMAGERY OF THE BIBLE

G.B. Caird

WINNER OF THE COLLINS RELIGIOUS BOOK AWARD

'An immensely rich book to which the reader will want to return again and again...All students of the Bible will find their understanding enlarged.'

Expository Times

'Learned, profound, exciting.'

Randolph Quirk, *The Times*

'Dr. Caird has a genius for selecting the apposite example, and for drawing parallels between texts. His commentary is learned and illuminating and never dull.' *Times Literary Supplement*

ISBN 0 7156 1579 3

A CRITICAL INTRODUCTION TO THE OLD TESTAMENT

G.W. Anderson

This clear and succinct introduction includes a brief history of the Old Testament Canon as a whole, and a detailed examination of each book or group of books within it. An account of literary forms and literary history, and a discussion of the place of the Old Testament in the Christian revelation complete the work.

'This is an excellently compact and informative guide. Professor Anderson has enabled the busiest teacher to keep up to date, and at the same time maintained a sober and balanced attitude to current theories.'

Times Educational Supplement

'His excellent book, in a short compass and with admirable clarity, reviews all the latest critical work on the Old Testament...a really judicious book which will become an indispensable text-book for some years to come.'

Church Quarterly Review

ISBN 0 7156 0077 X

A CRITICAL INTRODUCTION TO THE NEW TESTAMENT

Reginald H. Fuller

'The art of writing "special introductions" is aptly demonstrated in this volume. In less space than that accorded Feine-Behm-Kümmel, Professor Fuller has made careful selection from a broad base of opinion, to produce a balanced and unified picture of NT literary and historical-critical scholarship today. Ministers, teachers, graduate students, and scholars alike will find this artful volume critically helpful and theologically instructive.' *Journal of Biblical Literature*

ISBN 0 7156 0582 8